THE
AMBASSADOR
Two Hats. Two Presidents.

THE
AMBASSADOR

Two Hats. Two Presidents.

Carmen G. Cantor

ROSALES MAVERICKS PUBLISHING STUDIO

New York | Las Vegas | Guadalajara

Title: The Ambassador
Subtitle: Two Hats. Two Presidents.
ISBN: 978-1-959471-80-6 (English Paperback)
ISBN: 978-1-959471-92-9 (English Hardback)
ISBN: 978-1-959471-81-3 (English eBook)
ISBN: 978-1-959471-95-0 (Ingram)
Library of Congress Control Number: 2025908494

Categories: Memoir / Political Science / Diplomacy
Cover design by: RMPStudio™
Interior design: RMPStudio™ Team
Photography & Archival Images: Courtesy of Ambassador Carmen G. Contour
Editor: RMPStudio™ Editorial Division, & Hefling Media Group

ORDERING INFORMATION: www.Adriana.Company/TheAmbassador

This work is a memoir based on the author's personal experiences and recollections. Certain names, places, and events may have been changed for privacy or narrative purposes. While every effort has been made to ensure accuracy, the author and publisher make no representations or warranties regarding the completeness or accuracy of the content and disclaim all liability for any loss or damage arising from its use.

Limit of Liability / Disclaimer of Warranty:
The author and publisher have used their best efforts in preparing this book. They make no representations or warranties with respect to the accuracy or completeness of the contents and specifically disclaim any implied warranties of merchantability or fitness for a particular purpose. No warranty may be created or extended by sales representatives or promotional materials. The advice, strategies, and views expressed herein may not be suitable for every situation. Readers are encouraged to seek professional counsel where appropriate. *This book achieved Amazon Best Seller status in the Race Relations category on August 31, 2025, within the first 72 hours of publication. Rankings, including screenshots, are made available by the author on her official website.*

Printed in Las Vegas, Nevada, United States of America
Manufactured in the United States of America

Rosales Mavericks Publishing Studio™ | 1180 N. Town Center Dr., Suite 100
Las Vegas, Nevada 89144 | www.Adriana.Company

To the eternal fire within dreamers that keeps us going against all odds, and to my family, who always had faith in me.

TABLE OF CONTENTS

FOREWORD

When I first met Carmen Cantor during her tenure as U.S. Ambassador to the Federated States of Micronesia, I was struck by her authenticity and genuine commitment to understanding the cultures she served. What I didn't know then was the remarkable journey that had brought her to that moment, a journey that this memoir captures with vulnerability, grace, and strength.

Carmen's story is quintessentially American. She is the daughter of working-class parents from Puerto Rico who dreamed of becoming an astronaut, studied sociology when international relations wasn't available, and ultimately worked very hard to serve the public at the highest levels of government under presidents from both parties. But what makes Carmen's narrative truly compelling is how she carried her island identity with her every step of the way, using it as a bridge to connect with other island communities and people around the world.

The concept of "Sí, se puede" (yes, we can) threads through every chapter of Carmen's life like a golden strand connecting past to present. From her childhood in Mayagüez, where her parents stretched fifteen dollars a week to support her education, to the ceremonial halls of Micronesian feast houses where she was honored with royal traditional titles, Carmen has embodied this spirit of possibility even when the path forward seemed uncertain.

What resonates most deeply with me is Carmen's understanding that authentic leadership requires more than personal achievement; it demands bringing others along on the journey. Her commitment to people-to-people diplomacy, her respect for traditional cultures, and her ability to see connections where others might see differences reflect qualities that our world needs at this moment in history.

Carmen's memoir arrives at a crucial moment when we need stories that remind us of our shared humanity across cultural and geographic divides. Her journey from studying sociology to becoming a U.S. Ambassador and an Assistant Secretary illustrates that when we approach service with humility, curiosity, and genuine care for others, we can build bridges that seemed impossible to construct.

As someone who has also navigated the challenges of bringing one's authentic cultural identity into spaces of power, I am inspired by Carmen's refusal to diminish herself to fit others' expectations. Her story reminds us that our backgrounds are not obstacles to overcome but strengths to embrace and share.

The young girl who once dreamed of reaching the stars ultimately found her calling connecting Earth's most distant shores. In doing so, Carmen Cantor has given us a memoir that is both deeply personal and universally inspiring, a testament to the power of perseverance, the importance of cultural understanding, and the transformative potential of public service guided by empathy and integrity.

This is a story that will resonate with anyone who has ever felt like an outsider, anyone who has served their community, and anyone who believes that with determination and grace, we can indeed create the change we wish to see in the world.

Deb Haaland
Former Secretary of the Interior
United States of America

ACKNOWLEDGEMENTS

Thank you to all the audacious dreamers and people who inspired me throughout my life, from the beautiful shores and mountains in Puerto Rico to the many halls and trails I walked in Washington, DC, and in the Pacific region.

I am deeply grateful to my family for their unwavering support and heart throughout this writing journey. My husband Carlos, my daughters Ashley, Amanda, and Adriana, my dad Anibal, and my sister Zoraida especially deserve my heartfelt thanks for their endless encouragement and understanding during the long hours I spent writing.

To my mom: Though you are gone, your spirit lives on in these pages.

Equally grateful to my friends, teachers, mentors, and former colleagues for their insightful feedback and support, and for always being there to listen when I needed it.

Additionally, I'd like to extend my utmost appreciation to the esteemed individuals who kindly and thoughtfully provided endorsements for this book. Their gracious and sincere words mean the world.

To my publisher, Adriana Rosales, thank you for her invaluable guidance and expertise in reshaping my manuscript into the autobiography you now hold.

And finally, to you, the reader, *gracias* for joining me on this journey. I hope this book resonates, inspires, and ignites your imagination!

Quote

"In the end, it wasn't just policy or protocol that shaped me. It was also science fiction, soccer cleats, and the rhythm of joy. They taught me that harmony isn't found by standing still but by learning how to dance between all the roles we hold before the music stops."

- Carmen G. Cantor

INTRODUCTION

Writing a book never crossed my mind while growing up in "mi islita" of Puerto Rico, as my late mother used to call it. Support and encouragement from my family and colleagues motivated the pursuit of writing one, especially during my time serving as Ambassador in the Federated States of Micronesia and a few years later, while serving as Assistant Secretary of the Interior for Insular and International Affairs.

This autobiography shares a journey and aims to foster inspiration and personal growth. I hope it sparks the imagination of those who read it, provoking thought and igniting new ideas.

It's a "Sí, se puede" type of story.

It explores my life, focusing on my Puerto Rican roots, family, and the insights gained from 34 years in public service. It's a personal account of how I made it to the highest levels of the US Government, from the city of pure waters, Mayagüez, to Washington, DC and the Blue Continent in the Pacific region; from the Civil Service ranks to receiving presidential nominations from two presidents from opposing parties, to becoming an ambassador and an assistant secretary, despite roadblocks, but undeterred by challenges. It's a story about persistence, hard work, resilience, and heart.

May "The Ambassador. Two Hats. Two Presidents" connect with every reader, particularly women, islanders, and individuals who find themselves navigating a more challenging path to reach their aspirations, whether climbing the career ladder, shattering ceilings, or achieving personal breakthroughs.

WHAT IS SOCIOLOGY?

Wat do you want to be when you grow up? As a child, I was asked this question over and over. I certainly don't recall answering "sociologist" or "diplomat." I did not dream of becoming an ambassador for the United States or receiving a royal title from traditional leaders in the Federated States of Micronesia (FSM). I did dream about becoming a princess after watching on television, along with over 750 million people all over the world, the royal "wedding of the century" between Lady Diana Spencer and Charles, Prince of Wales, in July of 1981. But studying sociology, working in global roles, or receiving a royal title of my own? These were things I could have never predicted, nor could I have foreseen the unconventional route my life and career would take. When I was asked what I envisioned for my future, the answer to the question, without exception, was always the same: "I will become an astronaut and work at the National Aeronautics and Space Administration (NASA)."

Dreams of Space

In the 1970s and 1980s, I was an admirer of fantasy and science fiction books, TV shows, and movies: *Star Trek*, *Star Wars*, *Space 1999*, *Battlestar Galactica*, *Superman* … Futuristic concepts like space travel and extraterrestrial life offered escapism daydreams of traveling through unusual lands or jumping to hyperspace to visit new planets, "to boldly go where no one has gone before," as the *Star Trek* title sequence boldly proclaimed.

Such entertainment allowed me to dream of what might be possible, sparking curiosity in a young girl with limited means. I wanted to not only travel the world and engage with other cultures but also go even further, "to infinity and beyond," as Buzz Lightyear famously quoted in *Toy Story*.

My infinity-and-beyond journey began in 1968 in Perea's Clinic in Mayagüez, a coastal town with a Taíno[1] Indigenous name, located on the west side of Puerto Rico. My hometown is called the "City of Pure Waters," the "Sultaness of the West," or the "City of the Mango." It is renowned for its guava jelly rolls, or *brazo gitano*,

---

[1] The Indigenous inhabitants of Puerto Rico before European colonization.

made by Franco's Bakery since 1850; Fido's sangria; and my alma mater, el Colegio de Mayagüez, the second largest campus of the University of Puerto Rico system. Nowadays, it is popularly known for its impressive display of Christmas decorations in its city hall, near one of the most beautiful Spanish plazas on the island.

Line of Descent and Upbringing

My sister Vicky and I were raised by our parents, Anibal and Zoraida, in the El Quemado neighborhood, in the mountains, a fifteen-minute car ride from the town center. Dad was born in the town of Maricao, about forty-five minutes from Mayagüez. The son of Vicente Castro Galindo and Dolores Justiniano Santiago (aka Lola) and one of eighteen siblings (yes, you read that right!), he quit school in eighth grade because of the economic conditions in the 1950s. As a teenager, he was hired as a delivery boy at a flower and pet shop, where he had the opportunity to learn business skills. A few years later, he joined the Puerto Rico Army National Guard, where he served for nine years, and after his return from basic training in Ft. Jackson, South Carolina, he opened his own business, selling flower arrangements as well as pets like freshwater fish, parakeets, and hamsters. The store's name was Floristeria & Pet Shop

Balboa, named for the Balboa neighborhood where I spent most of my childhood.

My mom was born and raised in Mayagüez by her mother, Magdalena Ramirez (aka Malén). Her father, Olivo Laracuente, died in the early 1940s when my mother was still a baby. Mom was one of nine siblings. After graduating from Eugenio María de Hostos High School in 1963, she worked for a few years as a product demonstrator showcasing Cafe Rioja around the island, and as a dental assistant. She met dad in the La Quinta neighborhood, and after some time, joined him in the family business after marrying in 1964.

Having parents who each had so many siblings made me curious about my family history and genetic genealogy. Growing up, my mother was fond of saying that one of her great-grandparents was from Spain, but we had no way to corroborate the information. With Laracuente being an uncommon name, I knew there was more to be learned about my genetic and cultural heritage so in 2024, I did a home DNA test to learn about my line of descent. My top ancestral regions came back as 38 percent Spanish, 19 percent Indigenous Puerto Rican, and 17 percent Portuguese.

I was thrilled with the results. First, my mother's hunch about our Spanish heritage was confirmed. Second, it was heartwarming to learn about my other ancestors. Discovering that I have indigenous blood was especially unexpected and exhilarating. Nineteen percent is not a small number, and learning this result, in particular, was a profound experience that nurtured a stronger sense of identity, belonging, and connection to my cultural heritage. Yet, it also sparked a realization that the historical account of the Taíno[2] annihilation in Puerto Rico and the Caribbean, which many of us had been taught in elementary school, may have been incorrect. This realization led to my questioning the traditional narrative, encouraging new analysis and information-seeking. More recently, some scholars have argued that Taínos were not completely wiped out after all and might have intermixed with other groups. Who knows? While we may never have the answers, this moment made me realize that I could not take what I was taught in school at face value.

---

[2] Puerto Ricans are considered descendants of Taínos.

K-12 Schooling

For the most part, Puerto Rico's public schools are accessible and diverse. But in the 1970s and '80s, misinformation, along with lack of funding and inadequate resources, was a common issue. By today's standards, my primary school education would be considered deficient. Recognizing this and seeking a way to empower me through a better education, my parents signed me up for an informal, public pre-k program in the Paris neighborhood when I turned four.

The small local program was headed by Doña Mencha, a beloved teacher. Everyone from el barrio went to Doña Mencha's little school, including my sister Vicky, who used to hide under one of the tables because she didn't want to learn *la cartilla fonética*, the phonetic primer used to teach reading. Thanks to Doña Mencha's instruction, I knew how to read and write by the age of five. When the time came to attend elementary school, I skipped kindergarten and was placed in first grade.

I attended a string of public schools in the area: Francisco Vicenty and Federico Asenjo Elementary Schools; José Gautier Benitez Middle School; and Eugenio María de Hostos High School. These public schools had limited resources but were accessible to all income levels, encouraging diverse student populations. And despite the limited resources, these institutions were home to some wonderful educators: I have fond memories of Mrs. Justiniano, Mrs. Toledo, Mrs. Zapata, and Mrs. Plaza, dedicated teachers who fostered a love of learning and inspired my academic success.

Civic Organizations and the Civil Air Patrol

While attending school, I joined every organization or club available: Girl Scouts, Leo Club, Math Club … These experiences enhanced my social skills and built a shared sense of responsibility towards the local community in Mayagüez. I remember advocating for non-smoking in schools, raising funds for the Lions Club local Eye Bank, and performing in school plays with my classmate and friend, Erick Walker[3].

My participation in these youth organizations helped me develop leadership skills through community service and taught me early on that it's possible to enact change. The

---

[3] Erick and I were in the same classes from third grade to high school, and both graduated with a 4.00 GPA. He's a successful engineer, consultant, and chef, as well as a world-class traveler. Our friendship has stood the test of time and remains strong.

organization that had the most influential impact on me was the Civil Air Patrol (CAP).[4] In addition to teaching me about space and aeronautics (something I thought I needed to become an astronaut), CAP taught me important lessons on leadership. Through my six years as a cadet member, I rose through the ranks, earning the Billy Mitchell and Amelia Earhart Awards. At fifteen, I was selected to attend the Cadet Officer School at Maxwell Air Force Base in Montgomery, Alabama. A few years later, I was nominated for the International Air Cadet Exchange Programs in Canada and England, representing the United States. These trips exposed me to other cultures and ways of life and fostered a greater appreciation for diverse points of view. I returned from these overseas experiences exhilarated and with a renewed perspective.

College Decisions and Sociology Whispers

College guidance was scarce during my high school years. A student with the GPA, test scores, extracurricular activities, and financial need like mine could have received full scholarships from US universities, but

---

[4] The Civil Air Patrol was founded in 1941 to serve as the civilian auxiliary of the US Air Force.

regrettably, I lacked the academic advice to realize such possibilities. Additionally, there was no internet, so researching the possibilities myself was very challenging. With my astronaut dream still in mind, I opted to attend the engineering school located just 15 minutes from my parent's house, the Recinto Universitario de Mayagüez, also known as "El Colegio."

Shortly after returning from my CAP exchange experience in England, I started my college education, enrolling in the industrial engineering program. However, after taking a few courses, I began to question my decision. Was engineering what I really wanted to do? What did I want to do with my life? How could I figure it out?

My parents didn't have a computer, cable TV, or even a house phone, as there were no telephone poles in the neighborhood. We had only three TV channels, all in Spanish, which showed the telenovelas we often watched. Without the internet, this left me with one useful resource: the library.

As I navigated library catalogs while considering my future path, I learned about the social sciences and international relations. These areas of study seemed to be a better fit than engineering. However, El Colegio didn't offer a degree in international affairs, and the only university on the island offering such classes was Sacred Heart University, a private Catholic school in San Juan, three hours away from Mayagüez. This was not an option for me. My parents could not afford to send me to a private school, let alone one located so far away.

Since a degree in international relations did not seem likely, I started focusing my attention on the social sciences, which spoke to my lifelong curiosity about people, identity, and cultures. And after weeks of secretly researching the university catalog, I found my new major: sociology.

While I eagerly anticipated the start of my new degree track, I dreaded sharing the change with my parents. I didn't say anything for weeks. When they finally found out, pandemonium ensued! My Dad, a firm believer that education was key to our success, immediately questioned my decision: "Mi'ja, what on earth is sociology? What are you going to do with that?"

I explained that sociology is the study of social institutions and how people interact with each other, explaining that it aims to understand how society shapes human lives. It encompasses a comprehensive range of topics, including family, education, government, social change, and societal inequalities. As for my father's question about what I would *do* with my degree, the honest answer was that I didn't know. I just knew I was drawn to it and that I had to trust my intuition.

My answer did not convince him. He was angry at me for a long time.

Nonetheless, I went ahead and switched majors. However, I needed help covering college expenses. My tuition was paid with the help of a Pell Grant [5] award, but there were other expenses, like books, to cover. Finding a job was almost impossible, and my allowance of $15 per week barely covered gas and meals. Needless to say, I learned how to stretch that $15. I was a regular at Pizza Hut, where I would order a personal pan pizza and soda for $2.99, and also frequented food stands where I could get empanadas for a dollar or less. Thankfully, in my junior year, with guidance from the Director of the Social Sciences Department, Dr. Jaime Guterrez, I secured a

---

[5] A Pell Grant is a financial aid award for undergraduate students who demonstrate financial need. It's the largest federal need-based grant program for undergraduates in the US.

part-time job as a research assistant with the Sea Grant [6] Program, under the leadership of Dr. Manuel Valdez Pizzini.

In 1989, I graduated alongside my two best friends from college, Vivian Rios and Marisaida Mendez. I earned a Bachelor of Arts in Sociology, Magna Cum Laude, becoming the first member of my family to earn a college degree, a groundbreaking accomplishment that paved the way for a fulfilling future I had yet to even imagine.

Dad always knew that I wanted to become an astronaut, but he couldn't have foreseen the nontraditional path my life would take. I was not going to be a princess but would receive a royal title in Micronesia. I was not going to be an engineer but would become a diplomat. And I was not going to earn a degree in engineering, but in sociology. The day I became a US ambassador, he finally understood why I had changed my major in college, grasping that my initial choice wasn't aligned with my personal preferences.

---

[6] Sea Grant is a Federal-University partnership program established by the US Congress in 1966. Its purpose is to create and maintain a healthy coastal environment and economy.

In January 2020, right before my swearing-in ceremony in Washington, DC, I asked Dad: "Papi, what is sociology and what am I going to do with it?"

He simply smiled; he couldn't have been prouder of me.

BARBIE AND WONDER WOMAN

While growing up, I was never exposed to the symbol of empowerment for girls that American inventor and businesswoman Ruth Handler introduced to the world in 1959: a Barbie doll. The doll was more than a toy it was a symbol that girls could do or be anything. Through the many different versions, the Mattel figure represented strong, independent young women with diverse careers, tackling any issues or problems, no matter how challenging or difficult they were.

Why didn't I own this toy? Simple: My parents couldn't afford it. Their socio-economic status in Puerto Rico did not allow them the luxury of buying toys for myself or my sister Zoraida or Vicky, as I nicknamed her after she was born. They were working-class individuals with limited financial resources. Despite this, they provided us with something more important than material goods and toys: a strong foundation of values, rooted in unconditional love, supportive attention, and lots of encouragement.

Although Barbie and I were never acquainted, one year my sister and I received other toys that symbolized women's strength: "Bionic Woman" and "Wonder Woman," dolls that personified empowerment, sparked joy, and quenched my wish for a Barbie. [7, 8]

Vicky and I received the dolls as gifts on Día de los Reyes, Three Kings Day. [9] On January 6 of every year, we would receive our small presents after we had symbolically gathered grass and water for the kings' camels. This ritual replaced opening presents on Christmas Day. Although my sister and I didn't like the idea of waiting to open presents until the sixth, as it felt like an eternity, we now understand why our parents insisted on maintaining the ritual: They were determined to keep a Puerto Rican tradition alive—and they succeeded.

---

[7] A Universal Television series launched in 1976, The Bionic Woman was based on the adventures of Jaime Sommers, a young woman who almost dies in a skydiving accident and is rebuilt bionically, just like her former fiancé, astronaut Steve Austin from The Six Million Dollar Man.

[8] Wonder Woman is a DC Comics character created in 1941.

[9] Three Kings Day is celebrated in many countries, including Spain, Mexico, and Puerto Rico.

Today, Día de los Reyes evokes memories of childhood, bringing to mind traditions that my own family, my husband, Carlos, and daughters Ashley, Amanda, and Adriana have upheld. While we also celebrate Christmas Day, giving the girls gifts that Santa Claus brought from the North Pole (including Barbies), Carlos and I taught our daughters the significance and traditions of Día de los Reyes, too. [10] Carlos, who didn't observe the holiday growing up, embraced the tradition.

Carlos moved from Bogotá, Colombia, to Orange, New Jersey in the early 1960s. We met in Winter Park, Florida in the mid-1990s. His career spanned over three decades in the US Postal Service, handling a wide array of duties: letter carrier in New Jersey; customer service supervisor in Florida; postmaster in Chesapeake Beach, Maryland; and labor relations Specialist in Baltimore, Maryland, and Washington, DC. He is now enjoying a fulfilling retirement, playing lots of golf.

---

[10] My daughters, who embraced a blend of holiday observances during their formative years, learned early on that Three Kings Day is also known as the Epiphany, a Christian tradition that commemorates the religious story of the three wise men who followed the star of Bethlehem to bring gifts to the Christ child. They continue to observe the holiday now that they are in their twenties.

Getting to know Carlos meant getting to know his big, blended family: his parents, Carlos Sr. and Marina; his five siblings, Marta, Gladys, Ed, Richard, and Nelson; and his three children, Shannon, Carlitos, and Anthony.

Joining a blended family was an unexpected life event, and I learned that building deep and meaningful bonds with Carlos's family and my new stepchildren would take time and effort. I focused on shared activities and open communication. With time and patience, we all started to understand and respect one another's individual rhythms and boundaries.

Entering a new family dynamic involves navigating changes in roles, relationships, and assumptions, something you learn much in the same way a child learns about social roles and situations when playing with dolls. But no matter how much role-playing you do with a Wonder Woman doll, no matter how well you navigate changes, or how confident or strong you are (or try to be), you can't truly brace yourself for all of life's unexpected events. I certainly don't recall role-playing an illness with my dolls.

Shortly after my mother and father sold their business, my mother was found to have depression, breast cancer, and Parkinson's Disease. [11] Things you wouldn't typically consider when you play with dolls. The news was devastating. Our family experienced a wide range of emotions, cycling through the stages of grief: denial, anger, bargaining, depression, and acceptance.

My mother's illnesses required a major shift in roles and responsibilities. The family did what needed to be done. We learned about the conditions, started working on a support system, and began treatment plans. And when the time came to consider alternative assistance, we grappled with one of the thorniest issues we ever encountered in our lives: the decision on whether to relocate Mom to a care facility.

Many Hispanic families value family unity and emphasize caregiving, making them less likely to place elder family members in assisted living facilities. However, at eighty years old, Dad was not equipped to provide the care my mother needed. Adding to the challenge, their home wasn't set up to meet my mother's new needs. My sister and I both lived too far away to help regularly, so we had to consider other ways to support our mother's care.

---

[11] Parkinson's disease (PD) is a progressive neurological disorder that affects movement, balance, and coordination.

Relocating someone with Parkinson's disease to a new environment, whether assisted living or a skilled nursing facility, is a very difficult decision, one that requires open dialogue. Thankfully, we are an open, communicative, and supportive family. Grueling as it was, we knew it was best for both dad and mom. Mom was placed in an assisted-living facility about twenty minutes from my parents' home in Mayagüez, Puerto Rico, and lived there for almost two years before passing away in March 2020. Dad visited her every day.

Coping with Mom's illnesses and the subsequent loss was challenging and heartbreaking. Today, we think of Mom often and miss her dearly. She was a woman of few words, embodying the essence of an introvert, a quiet and soft-spoken soul. An incredible cook, she taught me the value of kindness, empathy, and understanding, and the importance of family, education, learning, and self-nurturing. If she'd had a Barbie modeled after her, she would have been a dental assistant, a career she often spoke about fitting for someone who prioritized self-care.

Luckily, my mother got to see my daughters play with the toys that both the Three Kings and Santa Claus brought them while they were growing up. She witnessed how

Ashley, Amanda, and Adriana developed their inner strength and self-confidence, so they could successfully navigate the world and thrive.

In contrast to my daughters, I did not grow up with many toys, but my upbringing in the beautiful hills of our neighborhood in Mayagüez represented a powerful blend of strength, courage, and empowerment. My mother and father raised me with the conviction that I could tackle any challenge, no matter how difficult, like learning how to swim at the age of twenty-one, acquiring the skills needed to handle a severe medical diagnosis, working my way up to two presidential appointments, or fighting against sexism or injustice.

I certainly never imagined that I would become a United States (US) Ambassador to the Federated States of Micronesia (FSM). Although I never played with a Barbie doll growing up, that didn't stop me from being inspired by symbols of empowerment: other dolls that represented problem-solving, independence, and the ability to overcome adversity.

I owe a lasting debt of gratitude to DC Comics, the creators of Wonder Woman, for having the vision and shining a light on what girls and women can do: anything.

Mattel has long inspired girls with Barbie's diverse professions, from astronaut to dentist. Will the doll's creator one day empower girls with an ambassador role model, Barbie? Time will tell.

SHAKING GROUND

As food products and merchandise came tumbling down, flying from the supermarket shelves, my gut reaction was to run to Dad and claim innocence. "I didn't do it! It wasn't me." No one was going to pin this on me. I was determined to set the record straight and ensure Dad knew that someone else, not me, was responsible for the mess in the supermarket.

Clearly, I did not comprehend what was really happening or understand the gravity of the situation. But Dad knew, and he immediately grabbed my hand and my sister's and ran out of the store into the street, where we sought shelter from falling debris and power lines.

My parents had already experienced plenty of earthquakes, a frequent occurrence in Puerto Rico. More often than not, the ground would start to shake while they were managing the family business in Mayagüez. Their store was in the Balboa neighborhood, very close to El Barrio París, about a ten-minute walk from La Plaza de Cristóbal Colón (Christopher Columbus Square).

I have many fond memories of growing up in Balboa playing badminton, marbles, *trompos* (a spinning top toy), and yo-yo with other children in the neighborhood; role-playing with my Wonder Woman and Bionic Woman dolls; and roller skating or skateboarding on the sidewalk, while daydreaming about becoming an astronaut. Ordering pizza and milkshakes from Pagliacci Pizzeria, eating roasted chicken and a fresh loaf of French bread from Chiqui's & Lourdes' Bakery, and getting Coca-Cola slushies from the store next to the middle school are all cherished recollections from my childhood.

But there is one experience in particular that will forever be etched in my mind: the time when Dad, my sister, and I were at Mr. Special Supermarket, and an earthquake hit without warning. This was my first time feeling the ground shaking. As a child, it was incredibly scary.

I vividly recall how everyone ran outdoors and moved to an open area, away from the buildings and power lines. Fortunately, there were no significant damages or injuries, just *el susto* (the fright) and the mess of scattered groceries I had been so afraid I'd be blamed for.

In the 1970s, people were not given the same earthquake safety training as they receive today, and safety techniques like "drop, cover, and hold on" were not the common knowledge they are today.

Sadly, this would not be the last time I would feel the ground shaking beneath my feet in Puerto Rico. I recall at least four other occurrences: at my parents' flower and pet shop in Balboa; at our home in El Quemado; at el Colegio, while pursuing my bachelor's degree; and in Aguadilla in early 2020, during the "earthquake swarm" of 2019-2020. [12] Again, luckily, no injuries or major damage occurred.

But this has not always been the case when earthquakes shake in Puerto Rico. My paternal grandmother, Abuela Lola, recounted stories about the earthquake and tsunami of October 11, 1918, a tremor with a magnitude of 7.2, with the epicenter in the Mona's Canyon, near Mayagüez. [13]

---

[12] The southwestern part of Puerto Rico was struck by what geologists call an earthquake swarm starting on December 28, 2019, progressing into 2020. It included eleven tremors of magnitude five or greater.

[13] The Puerto Rico Seismic Network lists a chronology of earthquakes in Puerto Rico dating back to 1615. The 1918 earthquake generated a tsunami that reached up to twenty feet high, hitting multiple locations along the island and reportedly breaking undersea cables, killing or injuring more than one

Abuela Lola was fifteen years old when the 1918 earthquake struck. She described how the ocean receded in our hometown of Mayagüez, exposing the ocean floor, reefs, and fish. People rushed to the newly exposed ocean floor to pick up fish, not knowing that a tsunami was approaching, with the water rushing back in faster and higher than expected, all the way to the viaduct, about a mile inland. Her words painted such a picture that they left an indelible mark: Every time I drive near the viaduct, I think of tsunamis and earthquakes.

I had the gift of having Abuela Lola in my life for fifteen years, but I never had the pleasure of meeting my maternal and paternal grandfathers, as they died long before I was born. And I only have a few memories of my maternal grandmother, Abuela Malén.

Abuela Malén never spoke about earthquakes or Barbies or Wonder Woman. However, I recall her playing with my cousin Norman (Tito) and me (we all lived in the same house for several years, before Tito moved to the town of Lajas), and discussing sports in particular, baseball.

---

hundred people, and causing $4 million in damage (in 1918 dollars).

Abuela Malén passed away a month before I turned five, in January of 1973, nine days after Puerto Rican professional baseball star Roberto Clemente[14] tragically lost his life in an airplane crash near the international airport in Carolina, Puerto Rico. She mourned Clemente's death as if he were a close friend or family member.

Watching professional baseball was very important to my dad, and he was instrumental in igniting my passion for the game. Every year, he would take my sister and me to minor league games of Los Indios de Mayagüez in the Isidoro "Cholo" García Stadium.[15] I loved going to the games, eating *pinchos* (marinated chicken on skewers) topped with bread or *tostones* (fried plantains), and responding to the call for cheers from *el Indio*, the unofficial cheerleader of the team. I still remember the

---

[14] In 1972, Clemente organized a relief mission for earthquake victims in Nicaragua. He decided to personally deliver supplies to ensure they reached those in need, tragically resulting in his death when the plane crashed right after taking off from San Juan. He was a Hall of Fame player and dedicated his life to humanitarianism and advocacy for minorities, particularly Latinos.

[15] The Mayaguez Indians are part of the Puerto Rico Winter Baseball League. Many revered major league stars played for Mayagüez, including Hall of Famer Tommy Laorda.

day Dad caught a foul ball from Jim Dwyer, a Major League Baseball (MLB) outfielder who played with the Indios from 1977-80. We went home excited and proud.

Growing up, I would play baseball with my cousin Tito and others near his house in the town of Lajas, but often, I would be called "out." It was not easy to make it to first base when you were one of the youngest players in the field and didn't know all the rules. As time went on, a deeper appreciation for the game developed (and the rules were learned).

Later in life, working in the Washington, DC area allowed me to fulfill my childhood dream of attending an MLB game. In 2005, when MLB owners established the Nationals (Nats) team, that dream came true, and I became a Nats fan and still am to this day. Although I have attended other professional games, I have never felt a connection to any team like I do to the Nats. Perhaps it's because going to games was a shared experience that provided a sense of community with my coworkers, friends, and family in DC. But it was about more than just watching a game. It was about sharing a passion with others. The Nats brought us together for me and for many others in Washington, too.

After having my own children, I wanted them to experience the same love for the game that I developed with Dad while growing up. When the Nats celebrated Star Wars Day, we were there. When they observed Roberto Clemente's day, we were there. Even my sister Vicky, her spouse Héctor Carlos, and son Gian joined us at games, along with Mom and Dad when they came to visit. The girls learned to appreciate the game and decided on their own which teams they would root for. Ashley and Amanda became Orioles fans, while Adriana became a Nats fan. Carlos is a Cincinnati Reds fan; I still don't know why.

Not all our family memories were shaped by fear. Some memories were marked by joy, and baseball was central to that joy.

Recently, I took Dad to a New York Yankees game in the Bronx and reminisced about our trips to the stadium in Mayagüez more than forty-five years ago, with friends and acquaintances from el barrio Balboa. Dad was giddy. This was his first time watching the NY Yankees live, and his first time at Yankee Stadium. He admired the stadium, its capacity, and the beauty of the game. We ate hot dogs, although I wished we were eating *pinchos*.

While in the Bronx, we did not have to worry about earthquakes, and I didn't have to do any explaining about items falling from shelves.

But, if an earthquake were to shake the ground again, and I was with Dad, I would remember how earthquakes taught me the importance of cherishing each day and the fragility of life. I know Dad and I would take cover under a table, not run outside like we did in the 1970s. And I will not worry about being blamed for products and items falling off shelves. I know *"I didn't do it; it wasn't me!"*

WHEN THE SKY BREAKS OPEN

Ashley, Amanda, and Adriana kept asking Carlos and me for a dog. Carlos often shared stories about Rusty, the German Shepherd he'd had as a boy, and I would talk about Charlie, the Pomeranian my sister and I had growing up. But after spending most of my childhood in my parents' pet shop, I was more than content with not having any pets for the rest of my life. I had spent so much time and energy taking care of the birds, fish, and hamsters at my parents' store. I was done. If the girls wanted a pet, it would have to be a goldfish; that was it.

Well, that's what I thought.

In the summer of 2010, Carlos showed up at our house with a box containing a little beagle pup, just a few months old, and I couldn't say no. She immediately stole our hearts. I will never forget how my daughters cheered and cried out with joy. They named her Nikki.

Nikki lived with us in Maryland for nine years. In 2019, Nikki moved to Cleveland[16] with my oldest daughter Ashley, now an adult.

Ashley had moved to Ohio in early 2018, after graduating from Florida State University in Tallahassee. She accepted a job offer from NASA at the Glenn Research Center, near Cleveland Hopkins International Airport. She moved there during the winter, and I still remember her phone calls, crying because it was "too cold" and "wouldn't stop snowing."

Nikki became a constant source of comfort and joy for Ashley, especially during times of stress or anxiety.

Needless to say, Ashley made lots of new acquaintances through her job at NASA, including her now husband Dr. Adam Gannon, a communications research engineer working on satellite communications. Adam might become an astronaut someday, and I will be there to

---

[16] While preparing for my departure for the FSM, I learned there were no veterinarians in the country. I was torn with the idea of taking Nikki to a place where she could not get medical attention, if needed, so I asked Ashley if she could keep Nikki. Ashley didn't hesitate Nikki immediately became her companion and emotional support animal.

cheer him on. Through Ashley and Adam, I'm living my childhood dream, vicariously.

My second daughter, Amanda, lives near Jacksonville, Florida, and works for the PGA TOUR as a Communications Manager. A graduate from the University of Maryland's Department of Communications, she has her dream job, where she manages all aspects of tournament communication, moderating press conferences and media engagement for players. She has worked closely with professional golfers like Rory McIlroy, Justin Thomas, Hideki Matsuyama, Collin Morikawa, and Max Homa, just to name a few. She even met Scottie Scheffler, the number one professional golfer in the world, on her second day on the job.

And here again, I'm living my dreams of becoming a somewhat good golfer through my proxy, Amanda.

My youngest, Adriana, is attending Northampton Community College in Pennsylvania, where she's pursuing a degree in fine arts. She's also working on a certificate program in Fashion Design Management from Cornell University.

Adriana is part of the COVID-19 student generation, the group who had to transition to online learning or hybrid models to mitigate the spread of the virus.

Per the National Institute of Mental Health Research, [17] compared to the pre-pandemic group, adolescents assessed after the pandemic shutdowns reported more symptoms of anxiety and depression and greater internalizing problems.

Adriana spent three of her four high school years taking virtual classes, without in-person social interactions. A talented artist, she faced several challenges, including mental health struggles, social isolation, and disruptions to her social life and extracurricular activities. As if this were not enough, Adriana also experienced something during the COVID-19 years that most of us will never come up against: a tornado, one of nature's most violent storms.

On September 1, 2021, Carlos took Adriana to register for her junior year at South River High School in

---

[17] NIMH, "COVID-19 Pandemic Associated With Worse Mental Health and Accelerated Brain Development in Adolescents," research highlight, January 26, 2023, https://doi.org/10.1016/j.bpsgos.2022.11.002.

Edgewater, Maryland. As remnants of Hurricane Ida caused bouts of severe weather on the east coast of the United States, an EF-2 tornado with wind speeds reaching 125 mph started ripping through Annapolis and heading for Edgewater. [18]

At the school, Carlos and Adriana received tornado warning notifications on their cellphones. The alert message instructed them to take shelter immediately, as a tornado was spotted on the ground, moving toward them. Everyone ran to the school basement and took cover.

I was in the Federated States of Micronesia while this was happening, separated by thousands of miles and a fifteen-hour time difference. I remember waking up to notifications on my phone about severe storms back home, as well as a number of text messages from friends and family. I immediately started searching for news on the internet and could not believe the devastation the tornado had caused. When I saw images of the high school stadium in Edgewater, my heart sank. I knew

---

[18] The Enhanced Fujita (EF) scale is a system used to classify tornado intensity based on the damage they cause, ranging from EF0 (weakest) to EF5 (strongest).

Carlos and Adriana had been planning to go to the school that day.

The tornado was two hundred yards wide, and it traveled over eleven miles for about twenty-five minutes. Carlos told me that when the danger was over, he and Adriana emerged from the school basement, along with everyone else who took cover, unhurt. They quickly realized that the tornado had struck the school, causing major destruction to the football stadium, the same stadium where Ashley and Amanda had played many soccer games during their school years.

Carlos drove home, not knowing that the tornado had also hit our subdivision on the South River, where it brought down trees and power lines, damaging many houses. Fortunately, unlike many of our neighbors, our house was not significantly harmed. A few trees fell in our yard, and our fence was slightly damaged, things you can easily fix.

But one thing you can't fix effortlessly is the psychological effect a tornado can have. Adriana can attest to that.

The tornado brought intense anxiety and depression. This, compounded with the effects of the pandemic, had acute negative effects on Adriana's mental health. The days after the storm were nerve-wracking, evidenced by emotional distress and issues sleeping. The shock of the experience led to feelings of fear, panic, and even numbness.

Thankfully, Adriana received medical care immediately, including therapy and medication, and was able to recover from the experience after a few months. It was not easy, but she managed to adapt well in the face of adversity and trauma, bouncing back from a very difficult experience.

In the process, she learned how to grow from her challenges.

Adriana is now flourishing. Our entire family is essentially living our artistic aspirations through her beautiful artwork. But we are also experiencing a whole range of emotions, including joy, happiness, gratitude, and a sense of appreciation.

While all this happened, our dog Nikki was four hundred miles away in Cleveland, unable to provide Adriana with the emotional companionship that could have reduced

her stress. [19] So, knowing the unique role dogs can play in supporting emotional and mental health and combating loneliness, Carlos and I made the decision to welcome another pet into our family.

In January 2022, a four-month-old Border Collie puppy joined our clan. Adriana named him Loki, after the God of Mischief in Norse mythology a very appropriate name because he is indeed the dog of mischief. Loki is Adriana's baby. He is extremely intelligent and has an intrinsic need to work and stay mentally stimulated, which is very beneficial not only for Adriana, but for Carlos and me as well.

I was not a big fan of having pets again after all the time I spent helping take care of the animals in my parents' pet shop, but having Nikki and, later, Loki, made me reconsider my feelings about pets. Having Loki following me around, nudging me with his nose, and wagging his tail in excitement when he sees me or anyone else in our family has brought forth a wide range of emotions:

---

[19] Nikki and Ashley had their own tornado experience three years later in Ohio, in early August 2024. Five EF-1 tornadoes ripped through Northeast Ohio, with the longest path running about seventeen miles. These storms caused widespread destruction and power outages. Ashley's car was damaged by falling tree branches, but luckily, they were unhurt after taking cover in their basement.

profound joy, healing through connection, and unconditional love. I never imagined he would become such a loved, constant source of companionship to Adriana and I will be eternally indebted to him. He has taught me the importance of healing, living in the moment, and not taking anything for granted, especially when the sky breaks open.

It's hard to believe a dog of mischief could do all that.

THE DAWN OF A CAREER

I vividly recall the events of Saturday, February 1, 2003, when the space shuttle Columbia, NASA's first orbiter to launch into space, disintegrated upon re-entry into Earth's atmosphere, killing all seven astronauts on board. The news reported that the accident occurred due to damage endured by the orbiter's left wing during the spacecraft's launch. The disaster underscored crucial shortcomings in NASA's leadership and organizational culture, decision-making processes, and safety procedures and measures. When the accident happened, my family and I were at Jesus the Good Shepherd Catholic Church in Owings, Maryland, attending my daughter Ashley's first holy communion.

I had been working in the federal government for almost thirteen years when the Columbia tragedy occurred. In my federal journey, 2003 was the year when I transitioned from a mid-level career position to a higher-level role as a branch chief in the Office of Civil Rights at the US Department of State.

At the time, the Department was under the leadership of four-star General Colin Powell, the first African

American to serve as Secretary of State. My boss was Barbara Spyridon Pope, a former assistant secretary in the Navy and an appointee of President George H.W. Bush's administration. Barbara led a very successful career, and I was very fortunate to work under her tenure.[20] She became an informal mentor to me, encouraging me to step out of my comfort zone and challenging me to explore opportunities for career development, continuous improvement, and personal growth. Her unwavering support taught me how important it is to foster solidarity, empower individuals, and challenge stereotypes. I learned that by doing so, you create a more inclusive and successful environment for everyone, both professionally and personally.

This was all new to me, as few people in my early professional life had taken the time and effort to help me navigate my career journey. I was not well versed in career planning and assumed that, if I worked hard

---

[20] Barbara Pope is known for chairing a committee to study the role of women in the military after the Tailhook scandal in Las Vegas, Nevada in 1991. Eighty-three women and seven men were assaulted during the event, per a report by the Inspector General of the Department of Defense (DOD).

enough, my career arc would lead me to a dream job at NASA.

It turns out, succeeding in a career isn't just about how hard you work, it's also about how you manage the journey. It's a dynamic process, with multiple phases and movement back and forth, up and down, and sometimes sideways. Controlling the trajectory of the journey requires networking, seeking continuous improvement, and never giving up.

The closest I ever got to fulfilling my dream of working at NASA came a year later, in 2004, when Barbara approved my participation in the Executive Potential Program (EPP), a federal government career development program.[21] The program required the completion of rotational assignments, with the goal of gaining exposure to divergent leadership experiences and viewpoints. As participants are responsible for securing their own assignments, I saw this as an opportunity to

---

[21] The Graduate School USA Center for Leadership and Management administers the EPP, a twelve-month competency-based leadership development program that provides training and developmental experiences for high-potential employees at the GS 13-15 levels or equivalent. The program theme is "Leading Change."

complete my rotational assignment at the agency I dreamed, as a child, I would work at: NASA.

My hard work paid off, or so I thought. I secured a rotational assignment in their Office of International and Interagency Relations (OIIR). [22] Their managers, however, wanted me there for six months, and Barbara could only afford to let me go for four. Our office was not fully staffed, making an absence of six months out of the question. Much to my chagrin, I could not complete the career assignment I had envisioned.

However... My dream didn't vanish; it just started shifting, although I did not realize it at the time.

Instead of the NASA rotation, I completed two assignments that ultimately became helpful in future jobs. One was in the Bureau of Consular Affairs at the State Department, working on American citizen services. This required consular training, which would prove incredibly valuable during my time as an ambassador in the FSM. The second was with The White House

---

[22] The mission of the OIIR is to provide executive leadership and coordination for all NASA international and interagency activities and partnerships, and for policy interactions between NASA and other US Executive Branch offices and agencies.

Initiative on Educational Excellence for Hispanics, a multi-agency working group within the Department of Education entrusted with strengthening the US' capacity to offer top-notch education, while increasing opportunities for Hispanic American participation in federal education programs. [23]

These experiences led to a deeper understanding of my values and gave me a stronger sense of purpose through my work. But getting to this stage in my career, which was a result of sustained efforts, dedication, and overcoming job challenges, didn't happen overnight.

My career journey embarked right after graduating from the University of Puerto Rico with a Bachelor of Arts in Sociology. My first federal agency job was with the US Postal Service (USPS), where I began working as a clerk, working my way up to management-level positions: supervisor of customer service, diversity development specialist, and federal women's program manager. Simultaneously, for two years, I pursued a Master of Arts in Labor Relations at the Interamerican University of

---

[23] Regrettably, web pages with information about WHIEEH's work went dark in January 2025 after federal agencies were told to comply with a White House order on removing certain language pertaining to diversity, equity, and inclusion.

Puerto Rico, while working the night shift full-time. After eleven years at USPS, I moved to positions in other agencies in the federal government.

In Washington, DC, I worked at the Federal Maritime Commission (FMC) as Director of the Office of Equal Employment Opportunity, and at the US Department of Agriculture, as Director of the Office of Civil Rights, in the Foreign Agricultural Service (FAS). These jobs were instrumental in developing my skills while learning about social justice and equality.

At the US Department of State, in addition to the positions I previously mentioned, I served as a recruiter [24] for the Foreign Service, and Deputy Director of the Office of Recruitment, Examination, and Employment during Diplomacy 3.0, one of the largest personnel expansions in State Department's history both in the Civil and Foreign Services. [25]

---

[24] This position was new, created in 2001 by Secretary Colin Powell under the Diplomatic Readiness Initiative to address the underrepresentation of Hispanics in the US Department of State.
[25] The State Department's archives describe Diplomacy 3.0 as "an ambitious multi-year hiring program that recognizes diplomacy as one of the three essential pillars of US foreign policy: diplomacy, development, and defense. To return diplomacy to the forefront in achieving foreign policy goals, Secretary Clinton has a plan,

Other positions at State included Director of the Executive Office in the Bureau of Counterterrorism; Director of the Executive Office in the Bureau of Educational and Cultural Affairs and Bureau of International Information Programs; and Director of Civil Service Human Resource Management.

These jobs equipped me with a diverse range of skills and cultural understanding and offered me the opportunity to learn about global issues and policymaking.

In 2019, I received the presidential nomination to serve as the US Ambassador to the FSM. My public service career concluded with another presidential position, this time in the US Department of the Interior, as the Assistant Secretary for Insular and International Affairs. This is where I learned about the importance of managing and conserving our nation's natural resources and cultural heritage, and about the federal government's responsibilities to American Indian tribes, Alaska Natives, and US territories.

---

dependent on continuing budget support, to increase the Department's Foreign Service personnel by 25 percent by the year 2013 with a 13 percent increase in Civil Service over the same period."

In all, I spent thirty-four years and seven months in uninterrupted service to the US Government.

As rewarding as these demanding positions were, landing or securing them was, for the most part, an arduous process and never straightforward. I still remember the many "After careful consideration, we regret to inform you …"-type letters I received after applying for positions, but I also recall the joy I would experience when I "got the call" with an offer of employment.

In particular, I recollect the moment I was notified I had crossed the threshold into the Senior Executive Service (SES), becoming a career member, and the privilege I felt after meeting and observing visionary and inspirational leaders at the Department of State or the Department of the Interior, some of them pioneers whose names will be forever engraved in our history books.

For instance, I had the distinct honor of working with Secretary of the Interior Deb Haaland and Secretaries of State Colin Powell, Hillary Rodham Clinton, John Kerry, and Antony Blinken. I also had the good fortune of working with resilient and decisive leaders like Ambassadors Tom Shannon, Nancy Powell, Ruth Davis,

Linda Thomas-Greenfield, Robert F. Godec, Caroline Kennedy, and Tom Udall, among many others.

The leaders I had the honor to work with were strategists and troubleshooters. But the quality that impressed me the most was their ability to empathize, engage, motivate, guide, and inspire their respective teams towards a common goal.

One of these remarkable leaders, Secretary Powell, used to say that leadership is solving problems. During his tenure, he focused on managing the "War on Terrorism," revamping US relations with Russia and China, and expanding international efforts to wage war against AIDS and nuclear proliferation. He was personable, supportive of his employees, and emphasized leadership every day. He successfully lobbied Congress for resources, creating leadership courses for the staff and getting full internet access on every single State Department employee desktop, not a given, in 2001. Before that breakthrough, if you needed to look something up online, you couldn't do it from your own desktop. You had to go to a special room, stand in line, and wait your turn to access the information superhighway, time-consuming and very inefficient.

In contrast, Secretary Clinton had a different but equally effective style of leadership.

In 2016, *Government Executive* magazine noted that "Hillary Clinton's leadership style combines feminism with a view that the government can accomplish great things." [26]

Highlights from Secretary Clinton's tenure include the opening up of Myanmar, tightening sanctions on Iran, her presence in the White House Situation Room when the operation to kill Osama bin Laden took place, promoting gender equality, and the liberation of Libya. [27]

In my interactions with Secretary Clinton, she always came across as well-prepared, determined, committed, pleasant, and fair. From the moment I observed her taking her own notes about something I had shared with her, to the time she spoke to students in the State

---

[26] Quote from *Government Executive*'s article "The Wonk in Chief."

[27] Per FBI.gov, bin Laden was a violent terrorist and mass murderer who used bombings and bloodshed to advance his extremist goals. His organization, al Qaeda, carried out the 1993 attack on the World Trade Center in New York City, the 1998 bombings of the US embassies in Dar es Salaam, Tanzania, and Nairobi, Kenya, and the September 11, 2001 attacks in New York, the Pentagon in Arlington, Virginia, and the plane crash in a field in rural Pennsylvania.

Department's Treaty Room and told them to listen to my advice, to another occasion when she made sure I was not left out from a group photo, I witnessed time and again how fair and gracious she was.

Nonetheless, perhaps the most impressive moment I witnessed while working with her was the way she handled the September 11, 2012, Benghazi[28] attack in Libya and its aftermath.

I saw Secretary Clinton on September 12, 2012. She was scheduled to speak at a Hispanic Heritage Month commemorative occasion with civil rights icon Dolores Huerta, but the program had to be canceled due to the gravity of the events in Libya.[29] In the midst of the chaos, Secretary Clinton remained composed, focused, and decisive.

Two days later, I saw her again at an airport hangar at Andrews Air Force Base in Maryland, at the ceremony returning the remains of the four Americans killed in the

---

[28] Members of the Islamic militant group Ansar al-Sharia carried out a coordinated attack against two United States government facilities in Benghazi, Libya, on September 11, 2012, resulting in the deaths of four Americans.

[29] Dolores Huerta is a civil rights activist who co-founded the National Farm Workers Association along with Cesar Chavez.

attack: US Ambassador J. Christopher Stevens and US government personnel Sean Smith, Tyrone Woods, and Glen Doherty.

I was in the hangar representing the Bureau of Counterterrorism, where I served as its first Executive Director. I will never forget the mix of emotions the ceremony evoked: sadness, disbelief, shock, vulnerability.

President Barack Obama and Secretary Clinton both gave remarks, but her words struck a chord. In her speech, [30] she stated that the victims' lives as well as those of all people who work in the Foreign Service "are at the heart of what makes America great and good. America must keep leading the world. We owe it to these four men to continue the long, hard work of diplomacy. We will wipe our tears and stiffen our spines and face the future undaunted."

We all listened and watched in silence as the four caskets were placed inside the hearses.

---

[30] Remarks at the Transfer of Remains Ceremony to Honor Those Lost in Attacks in Benghazi, Libya: https://2009-2017.state.gov/secretary/20092013clinton/rm/2012/09/197780.htm

Brushing away tears and stiffening the spine to face the future unafraid is not something most movers and shakers imagine they will have to do in their career journeys, but it is part of growing as a leader. I witnessed Secretary Clinton guiding her team during a very dark moment, reminding us of the importance of continuing the strenuous work of diplomacy.

I could never have anticipated that my career journey would put me in a front row seat to such moments of historic gravity. When the Columbia shuttle disintegrated in 2003, while I sat in church with my daughter, I had no clue that I would walk the halls of power and witness the quiet strength of real leaders firsthand.

But I know now: Leadership isn't about titles or proximity to fame. It's about who you become when the world calls you to rise and how you carry others with you when you do.

CAREER SUNRISE AND SEPTEMBER 11, 2001

Yes, leadership is definitely about solving problems. But it is also about vision, integrity, resilience, empathy, accountability, self-awareness, emotional intelligence, and being genuine. It is about treating people with respect, and it involves acts of kindness and empowerment.

In order to flourish professionally and build a fulfilling career path, one must cultivate not only the traits I just mentioned, among others, but also show a commitment to continuous learning and professional development. This is how you find a career that aligns with your passions and values, and succeed in leading people and change.

None of this was on my mind on September 11, 2001. Having worked as a public servant in the USPS for eleven years, I had begun to look at potential opportunities in other federal agencies. I was trying to align my career interests with specific organizations. Up until that point, I felt I had not carved a clear career path; I was just going with the flow. But change was on the horizon, although I didn't see it coming.

The day before the tragic events of September 11, 2001, I had an interview for a new position in the US Department of State. I was excited about the prospect of working in the oldest executive branch agency in the United States. Further, the mission of the State Department intrigued me. The Department advises the President of the United States and leads the nation in foreign policy matters. The interview marked my first time at the Harry S Truman building, aka "Main State," the headquarters on C Street Northwest in Washington, DC. After seeing the hall of flags in the main lobby, I was inspired. I then met with the interviewer, Diane Castiglione, the Recruitment Unit Branch chief, and left the building feeling I had performed well.

The next morning, around 8:30 am, while sitting in my cubicle in the USPS headquarters at L'Enfant Plaza in Southwest DC, I received a call from the Department of State asking me to return for a second job interview on Friday, September 14.

For a moment, I was euphoric, but my joy was short-lived.

At 8:46 am, sixteen minutes after my call with the State Department, American Airlines Flight 11 crashed into the North Tower of the World Trade Center (WTC) in New York City (NYC). Seventeen minutes later, at 9:03 am, I watched United Airlines Flight 175 crash into the South Tower of the WTC, live on television. After seeing that second plane, I knew this was no accident.

After the first two crashes, federal employees in the USPS Headquarters building in DC were advised to shelter in place, away from windows, as there were rumors of other unaccounted planes in the air.

At 9:37 am, American Airlines Flight 77 crashed into The Pentagon, the headquarters of the US Department of Defense, in Arlington, Virginia about three miles from the building I was sitting in.

The United States of America was under attack.

As the realization hit, my first thoughts were with the thousands of victims and their families. My mind then turned to my own family. I knew Carlos was at a dentist appointment in Suitland, Maryland, while Ashley was at school, and Amanda was at daycare, both in Maryland.

I drove home with a heavy sense of unease, another aircraft was missing, with reports that it was on its way to the US Capitol. United Airlines Flight 93 had been hijacked at 9:28 am, and no one knew where it was. Radio news was reporting a bomb near Main State, the same building I had just visited twenty-four hours earlier; this report was later proven inaccurate, all part of the chaos that unfolded following the terrorist attacks.

I attempted to reach Carlos by cell phone on my way home but couldn't get through. I also tried to call my parents and sister in Mayagüez, knowing they would be worried, but the network was overloaded. The attacks led to a surge in calls and data traffic, resulting in a failure of the cell phone network and widespread service outages. Hours later, I was able to reach one of my aunts, Aida, and asked her to relay to my parents that we were okay.

On my way home, I picked up Amanda, then three, from daycare, but decided to leave Ashley, six, at school. I didn't want her to see the news. Later that day, it dawned on me that I had made a mistake. Unbeknownst to Carlos and me, the school principal called all elementary students to the cafeteria for an announcement regarding the terrorist attack in the DC metropolitan area, with no consideration for the students' ages or the profound impact the news would have on them, especially since many parents were members of the federal workforce in the Washington, DC area.

With most of Ashley's classmates already picked up, my daughter couldn't help but feel that something had happened to me. Thankfully, this was not the case.

Nonetheless, the memory of not picking her up early still haunts me.

The September 11 attacks had a heartfelt and long-lasting impact on our country, leading to expanded security measures and a shift in US foreign policy. In the aftermath of the attacks, many Americans felt a stronger sense of civic responsibility and patriotism, and many were more inclined to contribute to their communities and country. And all this was happening at the same time; the State Department offered me the job to help recruit the next generation of diplomats.

A month after the September 11 attacks, I began working for the Department. As I traveled across the United States in my new role, I witnessed a renewed focus on public service, a keen sense of national unity, and a desire to give back. A wave of determination swept through the country and territories, inspiring people to act, and I was deeply proud to be a part of that.

It is during this time that people felt a need to take action and effect change that Secretary of State Colin Powell continued his efforts to reshape the State Department's organizational culture.

I, for example, started honing my leadership abilities and pursued jobs and career development programs that aligned closely with my interests and strengths.

This road took me to a few federal agencies and bureaus within the State Department. For instance, at the Federal Maritime Commission, I was selected to participate in the SES Career Development Program (SESCDP).[31] At

---

[31] The Office of Personnel Management describes the Senior Executive Service Candidate Development Program (SESCDP) as one succession management instrument agencies may use to identify and prepare potential senior executive leaders.

State, I had a position in the Bureau of Human Resources that helped me understand the financial and talent aspects of leadership, system wide. I pursued a position in the then-Office of Counterterrorism (which I helped establish as the new Bureau of Counterterrorism [32] a year later), and another position in the Bureaus of Educational and Cultural Affairs (ECA) [33] and International Information Programs (IIP) [34] as Executive Director, an SES position.

It was through ECA-IIP that I learned about the global reach of the Fulbright and International Visitor Leadership exchange programs, as well as the impact of Education USA, the Cultural Heritage Center, American

---

[32] The US Department of State's website notes that its Bureau of Counterterrorism works to strengthen partnerships, civilian capacity, and information sharing around the world to counter evolving terrorist threats and prevent the spread of violent extremism.

[33] ECA works to build friendly, peaceful relations between the people of the United States and the people of other countries through academic, cultural, sports, and professional exchanges, as well as public-private partnerships, as required by the Mutual Educational and Cultural Exchange Act of 1961.

[34] During my tenure as Executive Director, IIP supported public diplomacy efforts by engaging foreign audiences on US policy, society, and values through various media and outreach initiatives. IIP is now part of the State Department's Bureau of Global Public Affairs.

Spaces, the US Speakers Program, and Sports Diplomacy.

Along the way, I had a chance to work with individuals like figure skater Michelle Kwan, who at the time was serving as a senior advisor in ECA, years later becoming the US Ambassador to Belize. [35]

Although it looks simple when summarized in a few pages, my career journey wasn't a breeze. It took me years to figure out how to successfully navigate my professional path.

Further, while I worked with many genuine, caring leaders, I also encountered supervisors who failed to treat people with respect and kindness and did not see the value of empowering their employees. For instance, on more than one occasion in my thirty-four years of public service, I was forced to turn down a career development assignment because my supervisor would not approve it. Although I could understand some of the explanations for the disapprovals, other reasons felt awkward, even

---

[35] Michelle Kwan is a retired competitive figure skater, two-time Olympic medalist, five-time world champion, and nine-time US champion.

absurd, at times. Examples include a joint duty rotation [36] at the Central Intelligence Agency, [37] detail assignments in other Bureaus within the State Department, and a request to volunteer for disaster relief efforts in Puerto Rico after Hurricane Maria. [38]

Working under challenging supervisors can teach valuable lessons about what *not* to do in leadership.

Every time I encountered supervisors or managers who lacked essential leadership skills, I took notes and vowed to myself never to make the same mistakes. Instead, I focused on communication and empathy, fostering a positive work environment, even when I felt I had been

---

[36] The US Government Intelligence Community (IC) Civilian Joint Duty Program allows civilian professionals to rotate to other IC elements for a period of time, fostering collaboration and broadening their understanding of the IC community.

[37] The CIA collects and analyzes foreign intelligence and conducts covert actions. US policymakers, including the President of the United States, make policy decisions informed by the information they provide.

[38] Hurricane Maria was an extremely powerful and devastating category 4 tropical cyclone that devastated the territory of Puerto Rico in September 2017, causing widespread destruction, including an island-wide power outage, damage to infrastructure, and a major humanitarian crisis, with an estimated 2,975 deaths and lasting impacts on the island's recovery.

treated unfairly or denied opportunities for advancement.

I choose to learn, stay calm, and remain professional.

Despite the challenges, my experiences at the State Department mark a turning point in my career. This is when I began to truly excel at my work and when people started to see the value in my abilities. I came to realize that I needed to understand my own strengths, values, and goals, and find meaning in my work, regardless of the obstacles placed in my way.

I did not know it then, but these experiences were preparing me to lead with compassion and conviction in my future role as an ambassador.

At this juncture in my career, I thought the next stage in my path would be a deputy assistant secretary job at the State Department but my journey was headed in a very different direction, halfway across the world, something I could have never imagined in September 2001, when I first admired the flags in the lobby of Main State.

It has now been twenty-four years since the 2001 terrorist attacks, a day etched in my memory forever. The strong sense of civic responsibility and patriotism I felt after September 11, 2001, so clearly articulated by Secretary Powell's famous words about leadership and solving problems, became my guiding light.

After becoming a career member of the SES, I decided it was time to stop going with the flow and started charting my own professional course. That path that would take me around the world, allowing me to represent the United States at the highest levels, and enabling me to engage, learn, and solve problems with other cultures.

Looking back, September 11 didn't just change the world; it changed the course of my life. It reminded me that time is not guaranteed, that service is a privilege, and that leadership is a responsibility to be handled with skill and soul. That morning, I was just another working mother trying to balance family and work ambitions.

By nightfall, I knew my mission was greater. I would no longer drift. I would lead.

TWO HATS. TWO PRESIDENTS.

B ecoming a US diplomat or Chief of a Mission (COM) never crossed my mind growing up. Nonetheless, thanks to courage, hard work, smart career choices, and the guidance of honest, supportive mentors, it came to be.

My journey to becoming a US ambassador was atypical, different from that of my former colleagues and Foreign Service Officers (FSOs). And it was nothing like that of the fictional character Kate Wyler in the TV show *The Diplomat*.

While the Netflix hit is entertaining, relaying the story of an American FSO trying to manage both her tumultuous personal life and a prominent new assignment as the US Ambassador to the United Kingdom, I wouldn't say it's an accurate depiction of the realities of becoming a chief of mission.

The show is unrealistic in a number of ways.

Wyler's character, played by Keri Russell, is portrayed making vital decisions without input from her country team and with very little oversight. The bureaucratic process of the US Department of State is far more complex. The show depicts Ambassador Wyler taking action on the spot, without taking into account negotiations or guidance from her supervisory chain in Washington, DC. Again, a far cry from reality. Finally, the show further presents an ill-advised depiction of how you become an ambassador in the first place.

Yes, I know it is just a TV show, and I remind myself of this every time I watch it. Still, it's hard not to raise a brow when Wyler is informed that she is going to be the next US Ambassador to the UK without being nominated by the President of the United States, and fully vetted and confirmed by the US Senate, all within a matter of weeks. It fits the Hollywood scheme, but it's not the reality of the situation.

Real public service is about preparation, commitment, dedication, and teamwork. It is about serving the needs and improving the well-being of people and communities, rather than individual gain.

It is not a spectacle.

Unlike Kate Wyler's, my path to an ambassador position did not include powerful connections to any US President or members of the administration. There were no shortcuts, glamour, nightly cocktails, or a Winfield House with 35 bedrooms and 12 acres of land.

My journey from the US territory of Puerto Rico was quite different. Some people may even say that my odyssey was quite unique.

So how did it happen?

As a career member of the US Government's SES,[39] I had the honor of being nominated to not one but two Presidential-appointed positions, each one requiring US Senate confirmation, by two different administrations, in two different federal agencies. On July 17, 2019, I was nominated by President Donald J. Trump to be

---

[39] Per the Office of Personnel Management (OPM), the Senior Executive Service (SES) leads America's workforce. As the keystone of the Civil Service Reform Act of 1978, the SES was established to "ensure that the executive management of the Government of the United States is responsive to the needs, policies, and goals of the Nation and otherwise is of the highest quality." These leaders possess well-honed executive skills and share a broad perspective on government and a public service commitment that is grounded in the Constitution. Members of the SES serve in the key positions just below the top Presidential appointees. SES members are the major link between these appointees and the rest of the Federal workforce. They operate and oversee nearly every government activity in approximately seventy-five Federal agencies.

Ambassador Extraordinary and Plenipotentiary of the United States of America to the Federated States of Micronesia (FSM), and on March 11, 2022, President Joseph R. Biden announced his intent to nominate me to be Assistant Secretary for Insular and International Affairs at the US Department of the Interior in Washington, DC.

Two Presidents from two opposing administrations. Two different hats. One process.

For any presidential appointment in the US Government, there is a rigorous course of action that includes internal selection committees, security background checks, ethics clearances, financial disclosures, and so forth. This is in addition to meetings with the White House and members of US Congress, and testifying at a confirmation hearing before the Senate.

Ambassador's appointments, in particular, are largely a mystery to the general US population. Some people believe that campaign donors, friends of the President, and members of the US Foreign Service are the only individuals who can become ambassadors. This is not completely accurate.

In any given year, 60 to 70 percent of ambassador or COM positions are held by public servants, mostly members of the Foreign Service, but also by members of the SES from the Department of State and other federal agencies. The remaining 30 to 40 percent are held by political campaign donors or people closely associated with the President.

As a young woman starting my public service career in 1990, becoming a political appointee like an ambassador or an assistant secretary, under any administration, did not occur to me. Despite that, it happened—not once, but twice.

How did it come about?

In the US Department of State, when you cross the threshold into the SES or the Senior Foreign Service (SFS), you are required to attend a mandatory three-week leadership course for senior leaders. The Foreign Service Institute assigns a mentor to each course, and each student is obligated to complete a 360-degree leadership assessment, gathering input from their peers, direct reports, and bosses, in order to identify their strengths and areas for improvement.

I attended the course in 2014, one year after becoming an executive director in the Bureau of Educational and Cultural Affairs (ECA). My class mentor, Ambassador Donald Yamamoto, a seasoned career diplomat with three Senate-confirmed ambassadorships under his belt, pulled me aside and asked about my career goals. [40] At the time, bearing in mind the way the State Department is organized, with most high-level positions held by members of the Foreign Service, I did not see a clear path to higher-level positions, other than potentially as a deputy assistant secretary [41].

After a few minutes of discussion, Ambassador Yamamoto asked if I would ever consider a chief of mission opportunity. Like most people, mistakenly thinking that those positions were reserved for campaign donors or Foreign Service-types, I told him I didn't think I would qualify.

His answer opened a world of possibilities I never knew existed for public servants like me.

---

[40] Ambassador Yamamoto was the US Chief of Mission in Djibouti, Ethiopia, and Somalia.

[41] A deputy assistant secretary is usually a senior executive service or senior foreign service official in the US federal government who reports to an assistant secretary-type position.

Ambassador Yamamoto stated: "You have the exact qualities we look for when we make recommendations for ambassador positions. Your 360-degree leadership assessment is outstanding, and you should keep this in mind for the future. It is all about leadership." He then proceeded to explain the process the US Department of State follows when selecting candidates for COM positions, and encouraged me to acquire more senior-level experience and "throw my name in the hat" for the COM positions in a few years, when the time was right.

This revelation was mind blowing. It gave me a whole new perspective and inspired me to continue striving for excellence.

Shortly thereafter, I learned that in any given year, the State Department has approximately thirty COM positions available for career public servants and it typically receives about one-hundred applications for consideration. The process is rigorous: leadership assessments, rankings by regional bureaus, presentations and discussions with senior level officials, recommendations from the Secretary of State, White House concurrence, vetting and, finally, congressional hearings.

It is a very meticulous process.

Time went by and four years later, in April 2018, Ambassador Yamamoto reached out. He told me he was drafting the list of candidates he wanted to put forward for consideration for COM positions in Africa, and wanted to know if I was ready to throw my name in the hat.

I was honored and humbled that he had even remembered. He said he had been following my career and knew I was ready for this next challenge. Bewildered, I respectfully accepted his offer to include my name. He discussed a few posts in Africa and decided to put me on the Swaziland list. [42]

And that's how the tide started to turn.

Fast forward six months: The selection committee met and recommended my name for an assignment to a different Embassy, a country in the East Asia Pacific region, the Federated States of Micronesia (FSM), where I served for two-and-a-half years, after being nominated by President Trump.

---

[42] A landlocked country in Southern Africa, Swaziland is now known as Eswatini (formally the Kingdom of Eswatini).

Being assigned to a different posting was no surprise. A dear colleague, Ambassador Susan Stevenson, had warned me that something like that could happen. And I'm glad it did, because my time in the FSM was nothing short of incredible.

Surprisingly, this would not be the last time I would undergo a presidential nomination vetting process.

Unexpectedly, twenty months into my time in the FSM, opportunity knocked on my door again. In late summer 2021, I was asked if I would like to be considered for a nomination from President Biden to become Assistant Secretary at the Department of the Interior, under the leadership of Secretary Deb Haaland, the first Native American ever to serve as a US Cabinet Secretary.

Once again, baffled, and grateful, I accepted this honor and underwent the same vetting process this time, with a better idea of what to expect.

Every time a new US President is elected, the Partnership for Public Service, a nonprofit, nonpartisan organization in DC that advocates for building a better government, tracks close to 1,200 positions requiring US Senate approval. I never imagined my two appointments would be part of the Partnership for Public Service's tracking system.

Why not? Let's be real.

What are the odds that a woman from Puerto Rico with humble beginnings, a public school education, and no political connections whatsoever would be asked to serve not once, but twice, in positions requiring Senate confirmation by two different Presidents from two different political parties?

You might say my chances were almost as unrealistic as the TV show *The Diplomat*. The fictional Kate Wyler would have never guessed that someone like me would receive two US presidential appointments in her career journey. After all, she and I had different upbringings and career paths.

But Kate Wyler and I have similarities, too. Keri Russell's character is a lesson in pursuing opportunities. When she is offered an ambassador role, she takes it. And when I was given my chance, I took the opportunity, too, and seized it with both hands.

What the world may see as unlikely, I now understand as inevitable. Not because the path was easy, but because I chose to say yes to every challenge, every mentor, every moment that asked me to step into something greater. And so, while fiction might thrill with its speed and spectacle, real life has given me something more lasting: a sense of purpose built on courage, patience, and integrity.

Two hats. Two Presidents.

One journey that began with a quiet belief that maybe, just maybe, I belonged here after all.

As Walt Disney, a Hollywood visionary, once famously quoted, "All our dreams can come true, if we have the courage to pursue them." [43]

I did.

---

[43] Quote from American visionary film producer Walt Disney.

MEMORIES

The Early Years

Carmen 1970

Carmen 1969

First Holy Communion
in Mayaguez, La Quinta
1978

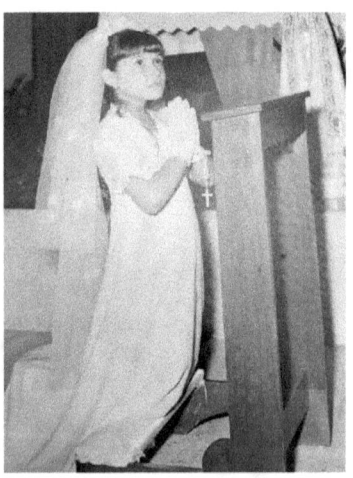

Girl Scouts 1977

Flower Shop
Balboa, late 1970s

Mom and
Dad, 1962

Carmen and Vicky,
early 1980s

Dad, Anibal
Castro, early
1960s

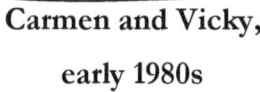

Second grade, 1974

Quinceañera 1983

Education

UPR Mayaguez
Graduation 1989

Carmen Cantor HS
Photo - 1985

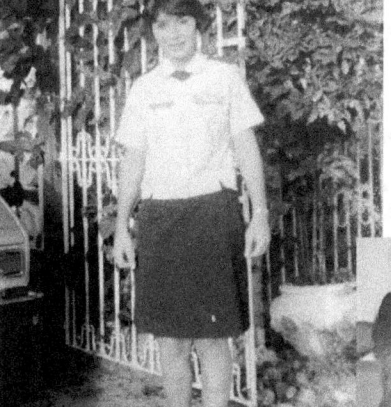

Civil Air Patrol,
1984

Elementary School
Graduation, 1979

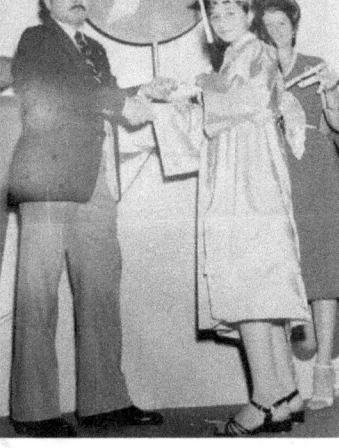

Alma Mater Colegial, Mayaguez

UPR
Mayaguez
graduation
1989

Mom,
Zoraida
Laracuente,
1963

Middle
School
Graduation
1982

Family

Family Photo, Cabo Rojo PR, 2016

Carlos and
Carmen
2019

Family
2025

Fun Family
Photo
2020

Carlos'
Family 2009

Carlitos' and Paula's wedding 2019

Family Photo

2019

Loki
Our Family Pet

The Castro-Laracuente Family 2012

Vicky and
Carmen
2019

Career & Service

Senate Confirmation Hearing 2022

Secretary Deb Haaland and Ambassador Caroline Kennedy

2023

Secretary Deb Haaland and Carmen G Cantor 2022

Mentor Ambassador Lino Gutierrez 2014

Palau President Surangel Whipps Jr. 2023

Secretary of State Colin Powell

2003

NASA Astronaut Jose Hernández 2024

Dolores Huerta and Francisco Palmieri 2012

Delia Garcia, Secretary Hillary Rodham
Clinton and Dolores Huerta 2012

INDOPACOM Commander Philip Davidson 2020

Army General Charles A. Flynn 2021

Eligible Family Members and DOD Staff 2022

Coast Guard Meeting 2020

Ambassador Linda Thomas Greenfield 2014

FSM President David Panuelo, Jan 2020

FSM COM residence with Chef and House
Manager Sammy Recites 2023

Official swearing-in Jan 2020

Ulithi Atoll, Yap, FSM

New
Zealand
Ambassador
To USA
Bede Corry
2024

Guam
Governor
Lourdes
Leon
Guerrero
2025

Senate Confirmation Hearing 2022

Congressional Hearing 2024

RMI President Hilda Heine 2024

Thailand
2024

US-RMI Compact Negotiations Meeting

US Embassy Kolonia team 2022

Pohnpei, 2020

Memorial Day 2022, FSM

Members of the US Compact Negotiating
Team

CNMI Governor and Lt Governor 2023

Dr. Anthony Fauci
Director, National Institute of Allergy and Infectious Diseases National Institutes of Health

Ambassador Carmen G. Cantor
U.S. Ambassador to the Federated States of Micronesia

Interview with Dr. Anthony Fauci

First day as
Ambassador
in FSM,
January 2020

FSM 2022

Snorkeling in FSM 2022

Bangkok 2024

Koror
Palau
2022

Swimming with sharks in Palau 2022

Ulithi Atoll,
Yap, FSM

FSM
USA
Embassy
2022

William
Shatner,
Captain
James Kirk
2025

Hayden
Christensen
Anakin
Skywalker
2024

PGA TOUR
Golfer Rafa
Campos

2025

PGA TOUR
Grand Slam
Winner Rory
McIlroy

2024

With mom and dad 2015

Hostos HS Classmates, 40th anniversary reunion, 2025

With Marisaida and Vivian, college friends

US AMBASSADOR IN THE BLUE PACIFIC CONTINENT

That phone call from late fall 2018 is still crystal clear in my memory. The phone buzzed as I walked to Columbia Plaza following a meeting at Main State. The voice on the phone said, "Carmen, you need to look at the map and find Micronesia. The State Department's Deputies Committee has recommended you to be the next US Ambassador to the Federated States of Micronesia."

I ran through what I knew about the FSM in my head. A young sovereign country in the western Pacific, an island nation that emerged from the Trust Territory of the Pacific Islands after World War II.[44] The country, comprising 607 islands across the Blue Continent a term used to refer to the Pacific Ocean had adopted its own constitution and became sovereign in 1979, and later

---

[44] The United States administered the Trust Territory of the Pacific Islands on behalf of the United Nations until 1978.

entered into a Compact of Free Association (COFA) with the United States. [45]

The call ended, and I was absolutely thrilled, honored, and grateful.

There I was, a public servant with no political connections, someone who had attended public schools in Mayagüez, being tapped to be an ambassador, a COM, representing the United States of America.

---

[45] The Compacts of Free Association or COFA is a unique set of international agreements between the United States and the FSM, the Republic of the Marshall Islands (RMI), and the Republic of Palau (Palau). It promotes economic and defense interests and allows citizens of the three countries to live and work in the United States. The US Department of the Interior's website notes that the United States and the FSM entered into a Compact agreement in 1986. The first financial package covered fifteen years, until 2001. Under provisions of the Compact, it was extended for two years while the countries completed negotiations for a new financial package in 2003, covering until 2023. A trust fund was also created to contribute to the long-term budgetary self-reliance of the FSM when the financial grant provisions of the Compact expired in 2023. The United States and FSM completed negotiations for a new financial package covering twenty more years in 2023. Under COFA, the United States provides financial assistance, defends the FSM's territorial integrity, and provides uninhibited travel for FSM citizens to the United States. In return, the FSM provides the United States with unlimited and exclusive access to its land and waterways for strategic purposes.

At that moment, I became the eleventh person and the third woman from the territory of Puerto Rico to be nominated and later confirmed as a US ambassador.

The vetting process began immediately. Hundreds of documents had to be completed: multiple questionnaires, ethics forms, l'agrément, [46] financial disclosures, and more. The process was very quiet. No announcements would be made until the White House had reviewed every piece of paper. It wasn't until July 17, 2019, that the official announcement was made.

Three months later, on October 16, 2019, I appeared in front of the US Senate Foreign Relations Committee for my confirmation hearing, along with four other nominees. The committee favorably reported my nomination to the Senate floor on November 20, and on December 19, I was confirmed as the next US Ambassador Extraordinary and Plenipotentiary to the FSM, by voice vote. [47]

---

[46] L'agrément is the process in which the US Government provides the name and qualifications of the potential nominee to the host country for a courtesy approval or agreement.

[47] The US Senate's website notes that the Senate conducts voice votes where the presiding officer states the question, then asks those in favor to say "yea" in unison, and those against to say

That night, on December 19, I was completely oblivious to the moment.

In true *Star Wars* fan fashion, I was in the movie theatre watching the release of *The Rise of Skywalker*. I had turned my phone off, and it was not until the movie was over, past midnight, that I found out my nomination had been confirmed.

A month later, I arrived on the island of Pohnpei. To get there, I traveled 7,695 miles, first taking United Airlines Flight 154, the "Island Hopper" [48] from Honolulu, Hawaii, to Majuro, the capital of the Republic of the Marshall Islands (RMI) before continuing on to Pohnpei.

On January 30, 2020, I couldn't believe I had finally arrived in my new home, the FSM, a country encompassing more than 600 islands and a million square miles of ocean, with four island states: Chuuk, Kosrae, Pohnpei, and Yap.

"nay." The presiding officer announces the results according to his or her best judgment. In a voice vote, the names of the senators and the tally of votes are not recorded.

[48] According to the December 2018 CNN report *Pacific Island Hopper: The world's most scenic flight?*, "aviation geeks call it "the holy grail of flight routes." For contractors, it's one of the world's most picturesque commutes, while for islanders across the region, it's a lifeline.

At the Pohnpei airport, I was welcomed by members of the US Embassy country team and a representative from the FSM Department of Foreign Affairs. After a brief meet and greet, I met my driver, Soster Robinson, a proud son of Chuuk, FSM, and was escorted to my official vehicle, an armored SUV, for the ten-minute drive to the Chief of Mission residence (CMR).

My new home sat on a cliff, overlooking the world's largest and deepest ocean. The house manager, Sammy Recites, was waiting for me with lemongrass tea and a batch of homemade cookies and brownies. Sammy had worked at the CMR for over 12 years, serving under four other US ambassadors before my arrival. An exceptional chef de cuisine, he took excellent care of the house, managed official functions efficiently, and cooked my meals for over two years. He also taught me how to make sushi!

The next day, on Friday, January 31, 2020, at 10:00 am, I officially presented my Ambassadorial credentials[49] to

---

[49] A formal ceremony, the presentation of diplomatic credentials occurs when a new ambassador presents a letter from their head of state to the head of state of the host country. This act officially recognizes the ambassador's authority in the country and marks the beginning of their term.

His Excellency, David W. Panuelo,[50] President of the FSM, in the FSM National Government compound in Palikir. I must admit, I had butterflies in my stomach. How often do you get to meet a head of state? How frequently do you carry a letter with the handwritten signature of the president of your country? The ceremony went off without a hitch.

In my conversation with President Panuelo, I shared my excitement about my new assignment. I noted the similarities between Puerto Rico and Pohnpei, and how I'd felt almost as if I were landing in Puerto Rico when I'd arrived. I discussed the willingness of the United States to defend the FSM against threats posed by transnational crime, terrorism, and illegal fishing in its 1.3 million square mile exclusive economic zone, and the shared goal of promoting a free and open Indo-Pacific region. In turn, President Panuelo reiterated his statement from his inaugural address, that the United States is FSM's closest ally and partner. He stated: "We are super delighted to welcome you to our country. With the wealth of experience that you do have, I am more

---

[50] Panuelo was the ninth president of the FSM, serving from May 2019 to 2023. Prior, he served in the FSM Congress from 2011 to 2019.

than confident that you will uphold our relationship between our two countries."

And I did. For the next two and a half years, I embarked on a mission to strengthen the relationship between our countries. On my first day on the job, I met with all embassy personnel, discussed the integrated country strategy, and explained my goals and priorities. With assistance from the country team, especially from the Department of the Interior, and some support from the US Agency for International Development (USAID [51]), we immediately started tackling education, health, and COFA economic issues. With the Department of Defense, we continued expanding the newly created Defense Attaché [52] Office, under the leadership of US Marine Lt. Colonel Erin Richter and later on, US Navy

---

[51] **USAID** was an agency of the United States government responsible for administering civilian foreign aid and development assistance around the world. It focused on promoting global stability, economic growth, and humanitarian aid while advancing US foreign policy objectives. In the FSM, Rodger Garner served as the USAID country manager during my tenure as US Ambassador.

[52] The Defense Attaché System is part of the Defense Intelligence Agency. Their mission is to **represent the United States in defense and military related matters with foreign governments around the world.** They operate from US embassies in more than one hundred locations globally.

Captain Tommy Price, two outstanding military officers I've been honored to work with. With assistance from the Australian and Japanese embassies, we collaborated on an underwater cable project connecting East Micronesia Island nations to improve networks in the Indo-Pacific region, where China was progressively expanding its security and economic influence.

Knowing that gender-based violence (GBV) was a major challenge in the Pacific Islands, with some countries having the highest recorded rates globally, I worked on raising awareness about the impact and prevention of GBV. As such, in partnership with the Pohnpei State Department of Health and Social Services, and the United Nations International Organization for Migration (IOM), [53] the US Embassy in Kolonia supported a campaign to stop violence against women. The initiative, #BlackoutViolencePohnpei, was very successful and the Pohnpei governor subsequently announced the creation of a hotline for victims and survivors.

---

[53] IOM is a United Nations organization working on the implementation of operational assistance programs for migrants, including internally displaced persons, refugees, and migrant workers.

Another area I focused my attention on was women's empowerment. At the time of my arrival in Pohnpei, the FSM was one of the few countries in the world with no women in its legislature. Understanding that I had an excellent platform to highlight how crucial women's participation in government is for social progress, economic growth, and overall societal well-being, I decided to act starting with supporting future female leaders. I spearheaded the establishment of a Girl Scout troop in Pohnpei, the first in the FSM in more than twenty years. With assistance from my contacts at USA Girl Scouts Overseas, we empowered more than thirty girls over a period of two years. Our Embassy's superb management officer, Somer Bessire-Briers, was instrumental in making the troop activities successful. Somer was also an excellent chargé d'affaires when I was not in-country. [54]

Supporting women empowerment initiatives was important to me but so was fostering trust and international cooperation, as well as encouraging open dialogue. Two of the most precious memories I have of

---

[54] A chargé d'affaire is a diplomat who serves as an embassy's chief of mission in the absence of the ambassador.

my time in the FSM include becoming a radio show host and participating in Operation Christmas Drop.

Unfortunately, due to the Coronavirus pandemic, limited flight schedules, and distances, I could not travel to many islands in the FSM archipelago.

How could I foster trust in a region where in-person connection was so limited? When discussing the matter with my team, they came up with the brilliant idea of hosting a radio show to reach out to the islands that we couldn't physically get to. We titled the show "American Waves," and it became the only radio broadcast done by a resident diplomat in the FSM.

The weekly show brought lively and engaging programming to FSM listeners and included high-profile guests. FSM President Panuelo joined me one week to highlight US initiatives in the FSM and talk about music (this is where I learned that President Panuelo is a huge fan of Elvis Presley)!

Another highlight, Operation Christmas Drop gave me the opportunity to witness first-hand the effectiveness of the Department of Defense's longest-running humanitarian mission, delivering essential supplies such as medicines and food to remote island communities in

Micronesian waters. The operation, which started in Kapingamarangi, Micronesia, in 1952, also serves as invaluable training for the United States Air Force and aircrews from allied countries, strengthening their preparedness for humanitarian assistance and disaster relief missions. In December of 2020, I flew in a C-130 Hercules, a four-engine turboprop military transport aircraft, as part of one of the missions. I will never forget the precision of the plane flying just four hundred feet from the water, and the joy the drop brought to the islanders. The experience was close to the way the Netflix movie [55] *Operation Christmas Drop* depicts the annual training exercise that takes place in Micronesian waters and the territory of Guam.

I am grateful I had the opportunity to observe the professionalism of our military service members and applaud them for their commitment to fostering international cooperation between our nations and allies.

I could describe many other experiences I had in the FSM, from observing the 75th anniversary of the end of World War II with leaders from Pohnpei to chatting with

---

[55] Netflix released the movie on November 5, 2020. It had a number of fictional elements but overall, depicted real events.

astronaut José M. Hernández[56] about education and perseverance or promoting understanding of the importance of our ocean on World Oceans Day. The July 2021 edition of *State Magazine* chronicles in more detail some of the work performed during my tenure.[57] But I would be remiss if I didn't mention here my work with one of the most impressive agencies in the United States Government: the US Coast Guard (USCG).

Given the FSM's size, fishermen and families are sometimes adrift at sea, requiring urgent, life-or-death assistance. During my time in FSM, the USCG conducted many maritime Search and Rescue (SAR) operations, saving several lives. They further promoted maritime safety by encouraging the use of personal flotation devices, painting boats orange (highly visible in a wide range of weather and light conditions), and implementing the use of emergency position indicating radio beacons (EPIRBs), a small electronic device that can help search and rescue authorities find people in

---

[56] José M. Hernández is a Mexican-American engineer and astronaut who was on the Space Shuttle mission STS-128 in August 2009. The movie *A Million Miles Away* is based on his story and describes his path to becoming a NASA astronaut.

[57] *State Magazine* is a digital magazine published by the USU.S. Department of State

distress. To assist, I presented EPIRBs to fishing tournament participants.

The USCG's work was nothing less than stellar.

In all, my time in the FSM was nothing short of amazing. The country is known for its unique cultural heritage, including high islands and low-lying atolls. The FSM has internationally acclaimed wreck diving sites and ancient ruins, including Nan Madol, the ceremonial center of the eastern Micronesian region and a UNESCO World Heritage site. Many of their citizens, along with citizens from the RMI [58] and the Republic of Palau, serve in the US Armed Forces in fact, they serve at a higher per capita rate than many US states, contributing to the nation's defense, and furthering their education in the United States, something many people in the United States are completely unaware of.

One element that became apparent to me early on is that the people of the FSM are very proud Pacific Islanders, and just like many others in Oceania, "do not want to be defined by the smallness of their islands, but by the

---

[58] RMI, Palau, and FSM are the only freely associated states with COFA agreements with the United States.

greatness of their ocean."[59] Being from an island myself, I understood this attitude well and took it into account in all the engagements and conversations I had during my tenure in the Micronesian region.

The moment in 2018 when I received the call to represent the United States in the FSM was a profoundly humbling moment. Being asked to go to another part of the world and work with Pacific Islanders, in a country with so many special ties to the United States, evoked a mix of pride and great responsibility. I'm particularly proud we connected through our common experiences as islanders.

FSM was just the beginning of a longer relationship with the Blue Continent. What began as an assignment quickly became a calling. In the FSM, I found not only diplomacy but also kinship, shared values, common histories, and a collective future shaped by trust. And though my time there ended, the lessons, connections, and gratitude remain as constant as the waves. I now know: every island, like every person, holds a greatness far deeper than its shores.

---

[59] Quote from Tongan and Fijian writer and anthropologist 'Epeli Hau'ofa.

PANDEMIC OF THE 21ST CENTURY

O n Friday, January 31, 2020, one day after I arrived in Pohnpei and a few hours after I presented my COM credentials to Micronesian President Panuelo, he decided to close the borders of the FSM [60] after hearing rumors of a cluster of mysterious pneumonia-type cases in Wuhan in China. This was about two weeks before the World Health Organization (WHO) announced the name of the new disease: Coronavirus (COVID-19). [61]

Receiving such dramatic news so soon after presenting my credentials felt surreal. The President must have had important reasons to make the decision. Why the urgency?

---

[60] At this point, the FSM border closure was not total. There were certain conditions for re-entering the country, including a quarantine of fourteen days in Hawaii or Guam, and a subsequent quarantine in the FSM. On March 14, 2020, after the President re-entered the country, flying in from Guam, the borders were permanently closed for fourteen months.

[61] WHO is an agency of the United Nations responsible for coordinating responses to international public health issues.

Throughout its history, the FSM has faced serious health challenges, including a significant burden of non-communicable and communicable diseases. Key causes of death in the country include coronary heart disease, stroke, diabetes, and chronic kidney disease. While life expectancy has improved over the years, the country continues to battle issues like poor healthcare access and a shortage of skilled personnel.

I immediately became concerned for the population of a country with such a fragile infrastructure.

President Panuelo knew that once the disease arrived in the FSM, there was a high chance the illness would spread like wildfire. In light of the FSM's regular travel connections to East Asia, and given the existing shortage of clinical resources, President Panuelo initiated border closures promptly to prevent transmission. As a result of his quick thinking and preemptive measures, the pandemic did not arrive in the FSM until July 2022, giving the country enough time to prepare.

Worldwide, the disease had far-reaching consequences, affecting people's health, means of support, and mental well-being. There was a dramatic loss of life, and estimates from WHO indicate that the total fatalities associated directly or indirectly with the pandemic from January 2020 to December 2021 was approximately 14.9 million. [62] The epidemic disrupted public health systems and created economic hardship around the world. And we all know the psychological distress caused by the disease and the restrictions it demanded, including anxiety, depression, and loneliness.

In the FSM, where the disease had yet to arrive, there were no country-wide requirements to social distance or wear masks, in contrast to the rest of the world. The FSM citizens were worried about the disease, but with the borders shut down, most daily activities continued as usual. I was perhaps one of the few ambassadors in the world leading a mission where everyone was reporting to work every day, and normal day-to-day operations continued, as if nothing was happening which we knew to be untrue.

For me, personally, much transpired during this time, starting with my mother's passing due to complications from PD on March 26, 2020, just two months after my arrival in the FSM. I was quarantined in the COM

---

[62] **WHO news release, May 5, 2022: "14.9 million excess deaths** associated with the COVID-19 pandemic in 2020 and 2021."

residence when my sister called with the sad news. I had re-entered the country with President Panuelo and others on a flight from Guam twelve days earlier and was required to complete a quarantine of fourteen days. When the call came, I was alone and would remain alone for two more days.

Losing a loved one, especially a mother, is a deeply painful experience. Losing someone at the dawn of a pandemic, amid so much uncertainty, was an experience unlike any other. To begin with, I couldn't travel to Puerto Rico. Flights to the island were dwindling, and there was no certainty about entry once I got there. The FSM's air traffic plummeted from thirty-six monthly flights to just one. No one knew when the next flight in and out of Pohnpei would occur. Furthermore, since my mother's death happened at the onset of the pandemic, it was unclear if the new disease had played a role in her passing. My father and sister were instructed to isolate themselves as a preventive measure, as it was uncertain if they had contracted the illness, too. Ultimately, it was confirmed that my mother had died from pneumonia, not COVID. However, this information came too late to spare my father and sister their period of isolation. Adding to the heartbreak, we couldn't have a funeral, due to the limits on social gatherings that had been put in place to curb the spread of the illness, and my mother was cremated, the first person in our immediate family to undergo cremation. [63]

At first, I was overwhelmed by a mix of feelings, but sadness and guilt were the most intense. I wasn't there to say goodbye, and I wasn't there to support my dad, sister, and the rest of the family. It was a truly heartbreaking moment, and I felt profound sadness and despair. In spite of all the sorrow, chaos, and uncertainty, I allowed myself to grieve and heal. I had no other choice.

My family and I decided to start honoring my mother's memory. We were not going to let her memory fade just because of the way things transpired. I had daily virtual calls with my dad, sister, husband, daughters, and other family members, during which we shared stories and reminisced about Mom as a comforting way to honor her. We also found solace in doing things that would have made her happy. She loved pepperoni pizza and

---

[63] There was an increase in cremation rates during the COVID-19 pandemic. Several factors contributed to this shift, including concerns about potential transmission of the virus from the deceased, especially during the onset of the pandemic when less was known about the virus and its persistence on surfaces.

Pepsi, so we had a day where everyone in the family, no matter where they were in the world, ordered pizza and had a Pepsi in her honor. Foreign Service Officer Somer Bessire-Briers, at the time acting as Deputy Chief of Mission, accompanied me to Arnold's, a small restaurant in Kolonia, where we both had pepperoni pizza in my mother's honor.

During this time, the embassy team was caring and thoughtful. They sent beautiful flowers to my residence and called the house to send strength and wishes for peace and comfort. Somehow, President Panuelo found out about my mother's death and called to offer his personal condolences. FSM Secretary of Foreign Affairs Kandhi Elieisar also called to express sympathy and support.

My mother's absence accompanied me through every silent moment of service. Although it was a difficult time, I made it a point to sleep, eat well, exercise regularly, process my emotions, and be patient with myself. I didn't know it at the time, but this would not be the only loss I would face while in the FSM. Two aunts, Carmen Lydia and Nilda, one uncle, Gilberto ("Lilo"), and my brother-in-law Ed also passed away during my first two years in the FSM.

These hardships were exacerbated due to the lack of in-person support from my husband and youngest daughter. Due to the permanent closure of the FSM borders in March 2020, my family was unable to physically join me. I wound up spending most of the pandemic in the FSM by myself. This was one of the most insurmountable things I've endured in my life, but we learned to manage it: early morning calls became the norm, and clear communication was key. We supported each other, and our family relationship became stronger, despite the distance.

While the FSM initially remained untouched by the pandemic, the disease's arrival seemed inevitable, so my work included helping the country prepare for this moment. The US Embassy in Kolonia, in coordination with the interagency, led US efforts to support the FSM during the pandemic. Key actions included adapting and expanding existing grant programs to provide assistance for pandemic-related issues like lost wages, shelter, and food distribution, as well as funding for testing and vaccination programs. Many organizations collaborated in this effort, including the Departments of the Interior, State, Defense (INDO-Pacific Command), Health and Human Services, Labor, and Agriculture, as well as

USAID and many others. The embassy hosted several vaccination drives with the goal of increasing vaccination coverage in Pohnpei and worked collaboratively with the FSM national and state governments to drive vaccinations and other public health programs. So many individuals contributed to these efforts more than I can name here. Captain Chris Chase, the commander of US Coast Guard Sector Guam,[64] was vital in helping the FSM reopen its borders in 2021, after coordinating a number of humanitarian flights from Guam. Meanwhile, medical epidemiologist Dr. W. Thane Hancock, from the Centers for Disease Control and Prevention (CDC), was instrumental in helping the FSM Department of Health & Social Affairs increase vaccination rates.

Nothing about this was straightforward or simple. We all can recall the widespread fear, swirling rumors, misinformation, and conspiracy theories at the beginning of the pandemic. There was also distrust from the public, which resulted in recommendations from international health organizations, governmental public health policies, and vaccine mandates being ignored because of limited information or fake news. At the embassy, we

---

[64] Now called US Coast Guard Forces Micronesia Sector Guam.

heard rumors about the FSM's apprehension to reopen its borders due to misinformation.

It was a trying time, with immense pressure, and I knew I had to take drastic action to address the misinformation. I was probably one of the few diplomats who thought to leverage high-trust figures to combat vaccine disinformation. Knowing that I had nothing to lose and a lot to gain, I asked the State Department to reach out to Dr. Anthony Fauci, one of the lead members of the White House's coronavirus task force, on my behalf and ask him if he would be willing to meet to discuss concerns the FSM had about the vaccines. To everyone's surprise, Dr. Fauci said yes. A few weeks later, he and I recorded a discussion that covered the virus, Pacific Islanders, vaccines provided by the United States, and how to achieve herd immunity. [65] In the days following the interview, the recording was viewed more than twenty thousand times. People of the Pacific Islands were thrilled that Dr. Fauci addressed their concerns directly. The FSM government made adjustments to its approach to fight the virus, publishing a press release

---

[65] Herd immunity is a phenomenon where a proportionate number of the population is protected from a contagious disease, which indirectly shelters those who are not immune.

expressing its pride in its partnership with the United States, helping to clear up misconceptions, and learning that these actions were lifesaving for many has been one of the proudest moments of my career.

Contributing to a more accurate understanding was rewarding, and moments like the meeting with Dr. Fauci brought positive feelings during a very tumultuous and sad time in my life. Over the course of my tenure as ambassador, I underwent seven preventive quarantines. In my free time, I worked on improving my tennis skills [66] (I still need a lot of improvement!) and learned why South Korean dramas (K-Dramas) are so popular in East Asia and the Pacific Islands. When I did not have to attend official functions after work hours, I would go home and watch K-dramas and compare notes with embassy-eligible family members Bonnie Chuang and Lorie Price, and Department of Defense staffer Jenn Lindner. *Crash Landing on You* and many dramas with actor Lee Byung-hun (known by many as the Frontman in Squid Game), opened a new world and culture to me,

---

[66] Tennis is widely played in the FSM. It offered me the opportunity to conduct "tennis diplomacy" with host government officials and members of the diplomatic corps.

helped me fight loneliness, and even learn some Korean. [67]

Fighting the spread of a global disease while coping with unexpected events like losing loved ones can be devastating if not managed correctly. Thankfully, I had great support from my family and team at the embassy, and for that, I'm forever grateful. Prioritizing my physical and emotional well-being, engaging in activities I enjoyed, and seeking social connections helped me grieve while maintaining focus. Grief is a personal journey with no single path, and there's no right or wrong way to experience it.

While working through my grief, I led the embassy team in Kolonia in supporting the FSM to prepare for and respond to the virus. We coordinated with US interagency partners, and the CDC engaged with the FSM to develop emergency response plans and support coronavirus testing. The country received supplemental funding from various US agencies and allocations of personal protective equipment from the national

---

[67] "Crash landing on you", a popular South Korean television series that aired during the pandemic, became the second highest-rated series in Korean cable television history in both viewership ratings and number of viewers.

stockpile. We collaborated with like-minded partners, including the countries of Australia, New Zealand, and Japan, as well as organizations like the Pacific Islands Health Officers Association (PIHOA) and WHO to address requests for equipment, medical supplies, testing, and technical assistance.

My mother would have been very proud of how I handled the challenges that came my way during the pandemic of the 21st century. I only wish she had been there to witness my accomplishments. But as I look back, I'm sure Mom follows my personal and professional success from heaven, with a slice of pepperoni pizza and a glass of Pepsi.

In the silence of quarantine, I came to understand something profound: Even in absence, love is active. And in every policy, I shaped, in every vaccine delivered, in every life protected, I heard my mother's voice. We were apart but never separate.

SWIMMING WITH SHARKS

I n 2009, the Republic of Palau [68] established a shark sanctuary, [69] the world's first, protecting its entire exclusive economic zone from commercial shark fishing. I was not previously aware of the designation when I first visited Palau in September 2022, roughly one month after I began serving as Assistant Secretary of Insular and International Affairs (ASIIA) in the US Department of the Interior (DOI). I had spent the entire day meeting with Palau's President, His Excellency Surangel S. Whipps, Jr., [70] and his cabinet ministers, discussing the relationship between our countries, economic and development cooperation, and shared priorities such as regional security, sustainable development, and environmental protections.

---

[68] Palau is an archipelago of over five hundred islands, part of the Micronesia region in the western Pacific Ocean, about a three hour flight from The Philippines.

[69] The sanctuary forbids all commercial shark fishing, including the retention of sharks caught unintentionally, and bans transactions involving shark products.

[70] Whipps is a businessman and politician who has been serving as president of Palau since 2021.

Never, in my wildest dreams, did I imagine I would get to spend a whole day with the head of a nation, nor did I fathom Palau would be the place where I would swim in the ocean with its guardians, up close and personal.

President Biden had nominated me for the assistant secretary position six months earlier, my second Presidential appointment in four years. Compared to the ambassadorial nomination, the confirmation process for this position moved quickly. I was nominated on March 11, 2022, and my Senate confirmation hearing took place on April 28. The Energy and Natural Resources committee favorably reported the nomination to the Senate on June 14. On July 20, I was confirmed by voice vote. On August 1, I was sworn in. The process was so fast, it took awhile for my appointment to sink in.

The DOI website describes the agency as "responsible for protecting and managing the US's natural resources and cultural heritage; provides scientific and other information about those resources; and honors its trust responsibilities or special commitments to American Indians, Alaska Natives, Native Hawaiians, and affiliated Island Communities." It also has a duty to conserve endangered species, among other environmental efforts.

I joined DOI at a significant moment: It was the first time a Native American had been appointed as a cabinet secretary in the history of the United States. I interviewed for the assistant secretary position with Secretary Deb Haaland, a member of the Pueblo of Laguna and a thirty-fifth-generation New Mexican, in October 2021. A deeply caring and fierce advocate, Haaland is one of the best bosses I've ever worked for. Few leaders inspire as she does. I feel incredibly fortunate to have worked with her.

As assistant secretary, I was responsible for carrying out DOI's responsibilities regarding the US territories, freely associated states, international technical engagement, and the oceans, Great Lakes, and coasts. I had made it a point to visit and meet with the leaders of the three COFA countries and the US territories under my purview. I knew that I would not earn the trust and respect of the territories and COFA states if I led from my desk in Washington, DC. It was crucial to be present and visible, especially in the Pacific Islands. I met the governors of American Samoa, the Commonwealth of the Northern Mariana Islands (CNMI), Guam, and the US Virgin Islands, and the Presidents of the FSM, RMI and Palau, all within my first six months on the job.

During this period, I also worked on strengthening the effectiveness of each office under my leadership. For instance, I focused on rebuilding the ocean team, supporting the ocean policy committee and co-chairing, along with NOAA, the United States Coral Reef Task Force (USCRTF).[71] The amazing team that comprises USCRTF helped foster partnerships, strategies, and support for local engagement to champion coral reef conservation, science, and management. In line with these efforts, I worked with local governments and the White House, participated in the Our Ocean[72] conference in Panama, collaborated with organizations such as Sail for Reefs[73] in Puerto Rico, and helped release baby turtles into the ocean in the US Virgin Islands. This last experience, in particular, evoked joy, hope, a sense of responsibility, and a strong feeling of empowerment.

---

[71] USCRTF was established in 1998. The Department of the Interior and NOAA co-lead the task force. It includes leaders of ten federal agencies; seven US States, Territories, and Commonwealths; and three Freely Associated States.

[72] Our Ocean is an annual conference that gathers governments, NGOs, the private sector and academia to identify solutions to key ocean issues.

[73] A local organization in Puerto Rico with the mission of providing a bridge between conservation of marine resources and water-based sports through education, interaction with the ocean, and habitat restoration work.

During my two and a half years at DOI, I also prioritized the work of the Office of International Affairs (INT), which is responsible for facilitating, supporting, and coordinating DOI's international engagement and US global policy objectives. INT was instrumental in coordinating and supporting Secretary Haaland's trips to Antigua, Australia, Brazil, Canada, Colombia, Namibia and New Zealand, [74] and my trips to Indonesia, Papua New Guinea, South Africa, and Thailand.

In Australia, for example, the Secretary highlighted the importance of indigenous knowledge, collaborative conservation, and international partnerships. The trip helped demonstrate the interconnectedness of the Interior Department's mission with those of international peers, including critical allies in the Indo-Pacific region. INT, the US embassy team in Canberra, and US Ambassador to Australia Caroline Kennedy played a key role in making this trip a resounding success.

In Thailand and Indonesia, I had the privilege of reaffirming DOI's conservation partnerships across Southeast Asia. For instance, in Bangkok, I joined US

---

[74] ASIIA's Office of Insular Affairs (OIA) supported Secretary Haaland's trips to Palau and the FSM.

Ambassador Robert Godec[75] to help launch the embassy's new "Virtual Jungle Thailand" campaign to raise awareness about endangered wildlife species, and highlighted successful US-Thai partnerships to counter wildlife trafficking. In Indonesia, I met with the Association of Southeast Asian Nations (ASEAN) Secretary-General Dr. Kao Kim Hourn to discuss shared environmental and climate goals, and traveled to Central Kalimantan to join officials from the Ministry of Environment and Forestry on their visit to Tanjung Puting National Park, a sister park of Big Cypress National Preserve in Florida since 2016, and home to the world's largest population of wild orangutans. This trip underscored the Department's long-term commitment to the region through the International Technical Assistance Program (ITAP),[76] investments in wildlife

---

[75] Robert F. "Bob" Godec is an American diplomat who served as Ambassador to Tunisia, Kenya, and Thailand.

[76] ITAP is part of DOI. It provides technical assistance to foreign countries, focusing on areas where the Interior Department has expertise, like natural resource management, environmental protection, and cultural heritage preservation.

conservation and protected areas, and partnerships with regional organizations such as ASEAN. [77]

In South Africa, I had the honor to be a member of the US delegation to the Intergovernmental Group on Earth Observations (GEO) [78] Ministerial Summit in Cape Town along with Dr. Rick Spinrad, NOAA Administrator, and Dr. David Applegate, Director of the US Geological Survey (USGS). During the visit, we participated in events of GEO's Executive Committee, plenary sessions, and several bilateral meetings with principals from South Africa, Paraguay, the United Kingdom and Australia. In addition, we highlighted the landsat program, a collaborative program between USGS and NASA that provides the longest continuous space-based record of Earth's land in existence. [79]

---

[77] ASEAN, headquartered in Jakarta, is an intergovernmental organization that includes ten Southeast Asian countries. Its mission is to promote economic growth and stability, and cultural exchange.

[78] GEO is a partnership of 115 United Nation member governments and 154 non-governmental organizations that work together to advance broad and open sharing of Earth observations globally and promote their utilization in decision-making.

[79] Since 1972, landsat satellites have continuously acquired images of the Earth's land surface, providing uninterrupted data to help

As my daughters would say, these trips were "cool." They were unparalleled experiences that gave me hope, a heightened appreciation for both nature and the work the US federal government does, and a sense of fulfillment. But the one country where I saw first-hand, more than in any other, the importance of conservation, and the impact and significance of our joint efforts, was Palau, the nation of roughly 17,000 people located in the West Pacific.

And this is also where I came face to face with seven blacktip reef sharks, an experience that inspired reflection on my expanded sense of self as a Latina leader, islander, and woman in federal leadership.

Palau is a global leader when it comes to environmental conservation. The country put into practice ambitious policies, such as the Palau National Marine Sanctuary, which protects 80 percent of its waters, and implemented a mandatory eco-pledge that includes a reef-toxic sunscreen ban. Palau also created the world's first shark refuge, before The Bahamas, Honduras, Maldives, Marshall Islands, and French Polynesia followed suit.

---

land managers and policymakers make informed decisions about natural resources and the environment.

According to *National Geographic*, the best way to see Palau is by water so that's exactly what I did when visiting the country. [80] On one of those occasions, I helped plant giant clams in the ocean with the First Lady of Palau, Valerie Esang Whipps (née Remengesau), and Bilung Gloria Salii, the highest-ranking traditional female leader of Koror State and leader of Mechesil Belau. [81]. I traveled by boat with Secretary Haaland to Peleliu, one of Palau's sixteen states and the site of one of the bloodiest battles of World War II. And with President Whipps, I visited JellyFish Lake, a marine lake on the island of Eli Maik, and the Rock Islands, several hundred small limestone or coral islands in the southern lagoon of Palau, a UNESCO world heritage site and a place of unparalleled beauty.

There, in the Rock Islands, is where unexpectedly, got to swim with blacktip reef sharks. I had observed sharks from boats in the FSM; however, Palau is the place where I shared the water with these guardians of the ocean, another once-in-a-lifetime opportunity.

---

[80] " *Why the best way to see the Pacific nation of Palau is by water,* "National Geographic, January 21, 2025

[81] A traditional women's group composed of women leaders representing each of the sixteen States of Palau.

As luck would have it, President Whipps had a GoPro camera and managed to record the encounter with the powerful animals. Although I experienced the most intense range of emotions, from an adrenaline rush to awe, I can assure you, the fear was there, 100 percent!

Witnessing these incredible creatures closely made me wonder about their power. But it also made me wonder which sharks were more dangerous, the ones in Palauan waters or the ones located 8,637 miles away in Washington, DC.

It's anyone's guess.

In any case, courage is about being present even when fear swims close. Isn't that what we call leadership?

AL GORE AND THE OFFICE OF INSULAR AFFAIRS

I was boarding a plane at Reagan National Airport in Arlington, Virginia, when my Chief of Staff Caroline Romano called to discuss an invitation, I had received for a speaking engagement. This was the second year in a row I had received this invite and regrettably, it looked like I wasn't going to be able to accept due to a scheduling conflict. She said the organizers of the event "really, really" wanted me there, but if I couldn't make it, they "would settle for Al Gore."

I stopped in my tracks and asked Caroline "What do you mean they would have to settle for Al Gore. Al Gore, as in former Vice-President Al Gore?"

Caroline said yes.

One of the organizational components under my purview at the DOI was the Office of Insular Affairs (OIA). This operation is responsible for carrying out the secretary's responsibilities for the US territories of American Samoa, Guam, the Commonwealth of the Northern Mariana Islands (CNMI), and the US Virgin

Islands. Furthermore, OIA manages and monitors federal assistance under the COFA to the freely associated states: FSM, the Marshall Islands, and Palau. I was asked to testify before the US Congress on matters related to OIA at least four times. The speaking invite stemmed from OIA's successful execution of a number of its initiatives.

These initiatives included the Interagency Group on Insular Areas (IGIA) annual meeting and the Territorial Climate and Infrastructure Workshop (TCIW). Every year, IGIA solicits information and advice from the governors and members of Congress from American Samoa, Guam, CNMI, and the USVI, and makes recommendations to the President of the United States, as appropriate, on the establishment or implementation of federal programs concerning these areas. TCIW hosts annual workshops bringing together climate and infrastructure representatives from the territories and federal agencies to discuss topics ranging from energy, broadband, and built infrastructure to invasive species and coral restoration. I was extremely fortunate to have the support of Julie Chávez Rodríguez, then a senior advisor to President Biden; Gretchen Sierra-Zorita, Director for Puerto Rico and Territories for the White

House Office of Intergovernmental Affairs; and Erika Moritsugu, Deputy Assistant to the President and Asian American, Native Hawaiian and Pacific Islander Senior Liaison to the White House. They were excellent partners during my time in DOI.

The four governors from the territories were also strong allies. They worked closely with me and my team to address obstacles within the federal system while also creating and implementing policies that addressed their own unique challenges. For me, particularly memorable experiences included learning about the tuna cannery challenges in American Samoa and assisting the territory with its economic situation; providing more than half a million dollars in assistance to Guam after typhoon Mawar in 2023, as well as resources to combat the brown tree snake invasion;[82] announcing funding to USVI to purchase medical equipment, educate youth, and train utility employees in energy grid management and integration across power sources; and representing the

---

[82] OIA provides funding and support for the brown tree snake program in Guam, which focuses on preventing the spread of this invasive species to other US jurisdictions, suppressing the snake population on Guam, and developing strategies for potential eradication.

US President as his envoy[83] for bilateral consultations between the United States and CNMI.

One particular experience from my time in public service that I will cherish forever is my involvement in the rounds of COFA negotiations between the US and the freely associated states. I had attended the initial phase of the negotiation process with the FSM in the summer of 2020 in my role as ambassador, and matters appeared to be moving forward. However, after the change of administration in Washington, DC, in January 2021, the negotiations stalled. RMI Ambassador to the United States Gerald Zackios ascribed the gridlock to Washington's neglect to designate a negotiator with authority to "discuss key issues beyond economic assistance, including remuneration for the legacy of nuclear testing on the islands, the presence of US military bases, and climate-change mitigation."[84]

I was still in the FSM when this was unfolding. I knew FSM negotiators were unhappy with the state of the negotiations and had heard through the coconut wireless

---

[83] This was a third Presidential appointment, fully vetted by the White House, but not requiring Senate confirmation.
[84] Reuters article: "With Blinken in Pacific, Marshall Islands says talks on *US* military access 'stalled'" - February 9, 2022.

the slang term used in lieu of "the grapevine" on the islands that the President of Palau was raising the issue at every opportunity. All three COFA states were disappointed, and the discussions had reached an impasse. Recognizing the importance of the three countries for US national security, Secretary of State Antony Blinken formally established a new position, a Special Presidential Envoy for Compact Negotiations. This happened shortly after Ambassador Zackios's comments. Ambassador Joseph "Joe" Yun was named to the position. [85]

Ambassador Yun and I started checking in regularly on matters related to the fiscal and economic policies of the negotiations, with an emphasis, in particular, on the oversight and accountability provisions of the agreement. He understood the intricacies of the agreements and the Secretary of the Interior's unique responsibilities in

---

[85] Ambassador Joseph Yun is currently serving as Chargé d'Affaires, ad interim, at the US Embassy in Seoul. He previously served as US Special Presidential Envoy for Compact Negotiations, US Special Representative for North Korea Policy, and Ambassador to Malaysia. He is recognized as one of the nation's leading experts on North Korea and known as the key diplomat who secured the release of American student Otto Warmbier in 2017.

administering and overseeing the federal assistance provided to the COFA states. To put it in simple terms, although the State Department handles foreign relations with the countries, when something goes wrong with COFA financial assistance, Congress defers to the Secretary of the Interior and the Assistant Secretary for Insular and International Affairs, not the State Department. Congress asked me about the Compacts multiple times.

During this period, I relied heavily on the knowledge and expertise of the DOI team. I informed Ambassador Yun that I would designate my deputy, Keone Nakoa, to manage day-to-day discussions with the three countries, with guidance from Melissa Braybrooks, Jonathan Dunn, Howard Hills, Steve Savage, and our attorney, Jeff Scott. The DOI crew spent countless hours, including nights and weekends, working with the team from the State Department to bring the negotiations across the finish line.

Or so we thought …

At first glance, the negotiations seemed to be back on track, nearing the endpoint. Unexpectedly, we had a few hiccups with two of the countries. Luckily, we were able to resolve these issues in a matter of months. Finally, almost two years from the appointment of Ambassador Yun as Special Envoy for COFA Negotiations, the renewed COFA were officially signed into law, with bipartisan support of the US Congress. President Biden signed the COFA Amendments Act of 2024 into law on March 9, 2024. The fruits of our combined efforts had paid off.

Words cannot express how proud I am of the DOI and State Department teams that worked on the negotiations, a genuine example of commitment to public service and our national security. These public servants understood that the relationship between the US and the FAS is rooted in a long history of cooperation and mutual benefit, dating back to the 1940s, and that this relationship is crucial for countering China's growing influence in the Pacific. Renewing the economic provisions of the COFA agreements was the correct course of action. I'm grateful for having been given the privilege to work with Joe Yun, Ambassador Karen Stewart, and the entire US team on this vital matter.

Working on COFA and in the Pacific Island region in general was truly an extraordinary experience. From the kindness of the Micronesian region's people to their beautiful cultures, it left a lasting impression. Having the opportunity to contribute to the area's economic development during a crucial time was deeply rewarding. Another highlight came when I was asked by the White House to join the presidential delegations attending the inaugurations of two new presidents in the region. In 2023, I was part of the delegation that attended the inauguration of His Excellency Wesley W. Simina in the FSM. [86] In 2024, I participated in the inauguration of Her Excellency Hilda C. Heine in RMI. [87] And in 2025, I attended the second inauguration of President Whipps in Palau.

My career has brought me great joy and incredible experiences. Meeting heads of state and having the opportunity to work with prominent public servants and politicians has left me awe-struck, more than once. But very few things have left me completely speechless. Receiving a call saying that if I can't make an event,

---

[86] Simina is a Micronesian politician from the state of Chuuk. He has served as the president of the FSM since 2023.

[87] Heine is a Marshallese educator and politician serving as the president of RMI since 2024, her second term. President Heine is the first woman to lead any sovereign country in Micronesia and the first person from the Marshall Islands to earn a doctorate degree.

someone would have to "settle" for the former vice-president of the United States? That left me completely stunned. Not in a million years did I imagine Al Gore would be my "backup" speaker.

At that moment, I felt like I'd truly made it in Washington, DC. When Caroline called, I was taken aback, unable to find the right words to express how I felt. Yet, after boarding the plane at Reagan National, I had a beaming smile the entire flight. I felt I had reached the pinnacle of my career.

To think that a young girl from Mayagüez could one day lead these types of conversations, influence US policy, and be considered a peer to names I once saw in headlines reminds me that even our wildest dreams can be exceeded when we serve with heart.

BAD BUNNY AND BELONGING

J ust when I thought I was at the peak of my career, after learning that Al Gore would be my "backup speaker," another famous individual burst my bubble and snapped me back to reality.

In 2024, I was privileged to receive a designation as the fourth Ambassador Edward J. Perkins Distinguished Speaker by Lewis & Clark College in Portland, Oregon. The speaker series was established to recognize the exceptional work of former student and life trustee, the late Edward J. Perkins. [88] Ambassador Perkins had served as a mentor to many individuals through his work with the International Career Advancement Program (ICAP), an initiative sponsored by the University of Denver's Josef Korbel School of International Studies. I had the honor to meet him when I participated in the program in 2012.

I was honored when I learned that Lewis & Clark College had decided to recognize my work through their speaker

---

[88] Edward J. Perkins was an American career diplomat who served as Director General of the Foreign Service and US ambassador to Liberia, South Africa, the United Nations, and Australia.

program. Abdiel Razo, my assistant in Insular and International Affairs, had just begun coordinating the details for the trip to Oregon, when our host called with concerns about the date of the speech. He was worried that the popularity of a well-known rapper who would be performing in Portland that same week would present major competition, impacting student and faculty attendance. I asked Abdiel who the performer was. His answer: Bad Bunny. [89]

Abdiel and I had had conversations about Bad Bunny previously. While I was not a fan of the lyrics of some of his chart-topping tracks, I appreciated the work Bad Bunny did in showcasing Puerto Rico, as well as his impact on diversity, equity and inclusion initiatives. When it comes to broadening global perspectives on these topics, particularly within the Latin music and cultural landscape, Bad Bunny has dismantled deeply ingrained stereotypes and brought marginalized stories to the forefront through his work in music, advocacy, and

---

[89] Known by the stage name of Bad Bunny, Benito A. Martínez Ocasio is a Puerto Rican rapper and singer known for breaking streaming records on platforms like Spotify, where he was the most streamed artist globally for multiple years.

activism. His cultural influence is so profound that Yale University is slated to teach a course about him. [90]

While Bad Bunny continues to effect change, something I applaud, words like *diversity*, *equity*, and *inclusion* have come under attack in the more recent backlash against DEI initiatives. But thirty years ago, the pendulum was swinging in a different direction. Many politicians, companies, and universities started valuing the unique perspectives diverse voices contributed, and began doing the work to ensure everyone was treated justly and a culture of belonging was developed. The need for this shift was pressing, a fact I was well aware of: In 1993, when I moved from Puerto Rico to the mainland, a former supervisor warned me that I would not be treated fairly because of my gender, ethnicity, and education level. While I didn't want to believe him, he was right.

Throughout my career, I was bypassed for promotions or temporary assignments a few times. Sometimes, positions were awarded to others with less experience or education than mine. There were times when I asked for feedback on the hiring process, and I didn't hear

---

[90] *NY Times.* "Bad Bunny (the College Course) Heads to the Ivy League," April 24, 2025.

anything, or if I did, I received explanations that didn't make a lot of sense. When one of my daughters, with no developmental or academic gaps was placed in a Title I class just because, per her teacher, I "spoke a second language and had an accent," and the principal revealed that the school was receiving grants that we, as a family, "fit" the criteria for, the words from my former supervisor echoed loudly in my head.[91] Neither my success and formal education nor my daughter's being an outstanding student at her previous school mattered. What was crucial, in their eyes, was our ethnicity.

I'm not going to describe every instance my family or I were treated differently because we looked or sounded a bit different. But I want this to be easy to understand: For individuals that share my background, the experience of discrimination is very real. It stirs up intense emotions, sometimes leading to a sense of powerlessness and helplessness, regardless of education or social status. Repeatedly, we have to essentially work harder than others just to be noticed, and still, we don't get

---

[91] Schools with a high percentage of low-income students (typically 40 percent or more) are eligible for Title I funds, a US federal program aiming to help these students meet state academic standards.

considered for opportunities or promotions. DEI initiatives help promote cross-cultural understanding, foster empathy, and ensure fairness and respect.

Colin Powell knew this when he was appointed Secretary of State, and made it a point to ensure employees were treated respectfully, regardless of the color of their skin, their gender, or national origin. Known for his humility, he empowered people and promoted initiatives that created a more inclusive workplace at every opportunity he had. Under his leadership, I was hired to help the US Department of State's Diplomatic Readiness Initiative, a recruitment program designed to build "a skilled, motivated, diverse and flexible workforce to better serve US foreign policy objectives and respond to international crises." [92] In March 2002, Ambassador Lino Gutierrez [93] and I accompanied Secretary Powell to an awards ceremony hosted by the League of United Latin American Citizens [94] (LULAC) in Washington, DC. Upon receiving LULAC's National Legislative Award,

---

[92] Excerpt from the FY 1999-2000 Department of State Performance Plan on Diplomatic Readiness.

[93] One of my mentors, Lino Gutierrez is a former US diplomat who served as Ambassador to Argentina and Nicaragua.

[94] Founded in 1929, LULAC is the oldest and largest Hispanic civil rights organization in the United States.

Secretary Powell spoke about the importance of making the US Foreign Service more diverse and discussed how I was helping the Department meet its responsibilities, a duty that I took very seriously. [95]

Standing up for equal treatment, defending human and civil rights, and advocating for democratic principles and global values, these principles are part of the fabric of America. This common ground has united our country's people and made America a beacon of democracy for decades. A dynamic civil society with heterogeneous and inclusive organizations and active public engagement promotes transparency and makes the government answerable to the people.

In my career, the first person who spoke out on my behalf to defend my rights was Postmaster Joe Rivera. Thanks to his vision, I was promoted to a supervisory position in 1994. He knew I had been bypassed for a number of positions, several times, and after noticing that hiring managers were focusing on my Spanish accent rather than my qualifications, he hired me. He said: "I'm looking beyond your accent. I'm going to hire you

---

[95] "Remarks Upon Receiving the LULAC National Legislative Award;" March 13, 2002, JW Marriott Hotel

because you are highly qualified, and have the potential and drive to move up the career chain and effect change." Joe was not afraid to remind others about different perspectives and how we are all interconnected, even though we have a diverse and often complex makeup.

Joe helped me learn how different perspectives enhance understanding and facilitate better decisions, especially when you challenge your own biases and assumptions. Listening to speakers who came to the workplace to discuss the importance of unique perspectives, like journalist Maria Elena Salinas, astronaut Ellen Ochoa, and civil rights advocate Dolores Huerta, also helped me appreciate different angles.

I know I would have not made it to where I am if it had not been for the support of visionary leaders and mentors like Joe Rivera. Joe is just one of many. Others who played a pivotal role in my career path include Felicita Sola-Carter, Sara Clemente, Elena Mola, Marisa Rivera, Francisco "Paco" Palmieri, and Javier Cuebas, as well as diplomatic trailblazers Ambassadors Lino Gutierrez, Ruth Davis, Arnold Chacón, Linda Thomas-Greenfield, Maura Harty, Luis Arreaga and Nancy Jo Powell. They provided guidance, support, and encouragement when I needed it, and helped me navigate challenges by offering trusted perspectives.

Mentors were not the only ones helping. Diverse organizations offering developmental opportunities and contributing to a more positive and engaged workplace played a key role in preparing me for increased responsibilities. The Hispanic Employee Council of Foreign Affairs Agencies (HECFAA), where I served as president for two years, helped me develop my strategic thinking skills. Also pivotal in equipping me for expanded leadership roles were The National Hispana Leadership Institute (NHLI); the International Career Advancement Program (ICAP); Friends of Puerto Rico; Grupo 21;[96] and the University of Puerto Rico Alumni Association (UPRAA). These organizations provided opportunities to connect with other professionals and helped me develop skills in analyzing problems and implementing plans to address them.

My work with HECFAA, for instance, led to my receiving the Department of State's Equal Employment

---

[96] Grupo 21 is a volunteer-based nonpartisan initiative led by stateside community leaders and elected officials of Puerto Rican heritage with a mission to support a diverse and inclusive Executive Branch.

Opportunity Award from Secretary John Kerry in 2015. These organizations were vital to my career: They provided a safe space for belonging, networking, career development opportunities, mentoring, and shared identity.

This brings me to my next point: On September 30, 2021, in collaboration with HECFAA, the National Museum of American Diplomacy website produced a piece entitled "Island Diplomacy, from Mayagüez to Micronesia: The Journey of Esperanza of Ambassador Carmen Gloria Cantor." As part of the museum's Hispanic Heritage Month series, the article highlighted my life journey from Puerto Rico to the Blue Continent, and my contributions to the United States as a career public servant. It was a beautiful piece that called attention to the value of uniqueness and different perspectives.

Heartbreakingly, on January 31, 2025, I disappeared. Federal government websites that contained the words diversity or gender started vanishing that same month, and my story, along with many others, evaporated from the museum website. It was replaced with an "Under Construction" page, and can not be found online, even in archived form. In February 2025, the *New York Times* reported that more than 8,000 web pages across government sites had been taken down. Melted away. Dissipated. [97]

Throughout my career, I used my platforms to elevate conversations about democracy and the American values of fairness, equity, authenticity, and helping others by paying it forward. I couldn't have foreseen that my own American story of hard work, loyalty, and resilience would simply fade away because of my gender or ethnicity.

The pendulum is definitely swinging in another direction. And I think Bad Bunny, in his wisdom, has been anticipating the swing change for some time …

Rearranging the Oregon trip dates to fit around a Bad Bunny concert was unquestionably a first for me. But knowing what he has done to promote fairness and an understanding of Hispanic communities, cultures, and social issues, I was more than happy to oblige. Bad Bunny has leveraged his platform to create awareness, enhancing the dialogue on the values of belonging and

---

[97] *NY Times* "Thousands of US Government Web Pages Have Been Taken Down Since Friday" by Ethan Singer. February 2, 2025.

respect. In the process, he has resonated with a global audience, galvanizing a significant population. He has reminded me to own my individuality and uniqueness, conquer fear, manage self-doubts, and not let the disappearance of my museum article defeat me. After all, as he sings "la vida es una fiesta que un dia termina" (life is a party that one day ends). [98] Why should I waste precious time feeling defeated or failing to understand the beauty of our diverse backgrounds? Instead, I choose to concentrate on our common humanity and the shared experiences that bind us.

I addressed the students and faculty at Lewis & Clark College in Portland on March 6, 2024; Bad Bunny performed in Portland on March 7, 2024. We both had full houses, not because he is famous and I wore two presidential hats, but because we belong, and we stand for something greater than ourselves.

---

[98] Album: *DeBÍ TiRAR MáS FOToS*; Song "Baile Inolvidable" (Unforgettable Dance).

A PARTY, GOLF, AND WORK-LIFE HARMONY

I agree wholeheartedly with Bad Bunny when he says that "life is a party that one day ends." And I, personally, want to live life to the fullest and have no regrets when my party is about to wind down. Throughout my life, I have focused on finding a rhythm where I feel fulfilled in both my professional and personal spheres, and embraced every experience. For instance, being a science fiction fan, I showed up at the pop-culture convention Awesome Con wearing a shirt picturing Darth Vader reading the book, *How to Be a Better Boss* and was unrepentant when I met *Star Wars* actor Hayden Christensen (Anakin Skywalker/Darth Vader). At Fan Expo Philadelphia, I wore a Starfleet officer uniform when I met *Star Trek* actor William Shatner (Captain James T. Kirk). Both characters were leaders, although one turned to the dark side. You all know who.

Finding fulfillment sometimes felt like going from the light side to the dark side of the *Star Wars* Force.[99]

---

[99] The Force is an energy field that binds the universe, connecting all living things. The light side of the Force represents balance,

Balancing the demands between my personal and work life while maintaining my overall health and pursuing hobbies I enjoyed was not a simple task. But although finding this middle ground was complicated at times, I never lost sight of my goal to live life to the fullest. I made it a point to dedicate time to my family, passions, hobbies, personal interests, and relationships, while also meeting my professional responsibilities.

How did I do it? When I look back, I sometimes wonder how I commuted an hour each way every day from the Annapolis, Maryland area to the Foggy Bottom side of Washington, DC, and back again. How did I manage to work a full-time job that included domestic and international travel while making sure my three daughters performed well at school, played competitive soccer, and served as Girl Scouts? And amidst all that, how did I manage to simultaneously give back to the community and find time for my personal interests? How did I manage to prioritize the things that brought me joy and helped me feel fulfilled?

---

harmony, love, and compassion, while the dark side stands for anger, fear, desire for power, and selfishness.

I have always been a driven individual. Yes, I achieved work-life harmony thanks to organizational skills, discipline, great communication, and a very, very supportive spouse. But I also used one simple tool: a wall calendar, or what I secretly called "The Kitchen Command Center." This paper calendar hanging in the kitchen, an area where my family spent time every single day, provided a visual representation of our schedules: doctor's appointments, soccer practices, Girl Scout meetings, work travel … It was all there. The calendar allowed us to see if we were overcommitted and needed to make adjustments, helped us deconflict schedules, and taught my family time management, a vital skill if your extended family is scattered throughout Puerto Rico, New Jersey, and Florida. Thanks to that calendar, we succeeded for the most part.

Of course, we had moments when things didn't go as planned, like the day Carlos went to pick up Ashley from soccer and ended up driving away without her because he was thinking about groceries. Ashley had placed her bag in the trunk of the vehicle; Carlos thought she had gotten in the car and started driving. The soccer coach called me to say it was quite a scene: Carlos driving away and Ashley running behind the car. He turned around when he noticed she was missing.

As much as we giggle about this story now, the reality is that those years were challenging, and balancing our jobs and family commitments was difficult.

When the "Runaway Dad" episode took place, Ashley was a freshman in high school, Amanda was in middle school, and Adriana in elementary school. Carlos was working in Baltimore, about forty-five minutes from our home in the Annapolis area, and I was in Washington, DC. All three daughters had soccer practices and Girl Scouts meetings several times each week. I would leave for work around 6:00 am every day and depart the office around 5:00 pm, depending on soccer practice or meeting schedules. Weekends were spent juggling soccer games, church, and other activities. I recall working on a briefing paper for an event with Secretary Colin Powell and Spanish opera singer Plácido Domingo in my car, while Amanda was at soccer practice. I also took calls from the Secretary of State's Executive Office on a Saturday at a soccer game, and handled an emergency call from the Department of State's Operations Center on Christmas Eve. No, these were not everyday occurrences. With time, I learned to manage these special circumstances, handling both work and personal engagements without problems.

Setting boundaries and making time for myself was also challenging but necessary. When the Department of State offered the option of participating in a pilot program to allow work email access on personal phones, I declined. I knew drawing a line between my personal life and work would be more complicated if all my emails were accessed from one phone. So, as inconvenient as it was to carry two phones at all times, I gladly did, for many years. That clear, necessary separation was worth it and allowed me time to do things I wanted to do during my free time, like giving back to the community as a Girl Scouts troop leader or "Cookie Mom," and as a board member of community organizations. It also allowed me to branch out and do things to decompress from the day-to-day activities, such as reading, going to concerts, traveling with the family, watching movies, or exercising, which boosted my self-esteem and helped me wind down.

Now that I have retired from public service, I'm chasing new pastimes. Golf, for instance, has become my new favorite sport. I play with Carlos when I have a chance. My main measure of success is making sure I don't lose as many balls as he does, but he's definitely a better player than I am. I started attending PGA Tour events; binge-watched *Full Swing, a Netflix documentary series about men's professional golf*; and became a fan of players like Puerto Rican golfer Rafael "Rafa" Campos, whom I had the honor to meet at The Players Championship at TPC Sawgrass, and the Northern Irishman Rory McIlroy, the number two player in the world. Perhaps what made me follow these two players, in particular, is their approach to work-life harmony and chasing aspirations. Both men personify perseverance. They have made their families, goals, and mental health priorities. And, like many of us, they have struggled with balancing work and family life.

Over time, I learned that what sets golf champions and successful leaders apart is their ability to stay grounded while pursuing work-life harmony, all while embodying grit and a drive to achieve their goals. It's refreshing to learn that Rory, for example, would unwind and recharge the night before his tournaments by watching *The Devil Wears Prada* or *Bridgerton*.

Watching a movie or using a paper calendar are tricks that might not work for everyone. But making time for yourself and doing things that make you happy will most likely bring joy and harmony to your life. It did for me. I could sense greater peace and fulfillment when I took my daughters to the Women's World Cup in Canada or to see Justin Bieber or Taylor Swift in concert. Going to Disney World's Galaxy's Edge at Hollywood Studios in Florida on opening week made me happy, and engaging in conversations with athletes like golf pro Rafa Campos, baseball player Pete Rose, boxer Larry Holmes, or soccer player Judy Foudy, people I never anticipated meeting, cheered me up.

Sports, science fiction, books, movies, television, and community organizations helped me decompress and achieve balance throughout life. They lit up my imagination and widened my view of what was possible. I don't know which famous pop culture character or athlete I will meet next, nor do I know what I will be wearing. But I do know that I will be having fun, engaging in activities that bring me joy, and feeling sunshine in my soul; in short, I'll be embracing the dance of life before the party ends.

In the end, it wasn't just policy or protocol that shaped me. It was also science fiction, soccer cleats, and the rhythm of joy. They taught me that harmony isn't found by standing still but by learning how to dance between all the roles we hold before the music stops.

CAREER SUNSET: "SÍ, SE PUEDE"

Dolores Huerta was in my office, waiting to see Secretary Clinton. This was not part of the plan. The women had been scheduled to meet earlier in the day, but plans had changed, so I unexpectedly found myself spending time with this courageous, passionate labor leader and civil rights advocate. The legendary figure who had coined the phrase "Sí, se puede!," was sitting across from me.

For a large number of people, myself included, "Sí, se puede" ("Yes, we can") is a source of inspiration and hope. Dolores is credited with coining the phrase when Cesar Chavez was fasting while advocating for better working conditions for farm workers. In the 1970s, it played a role in transforming farmworkers' challenges into an ethical issue that received country-wide support in the United States. The phrase continues to embody a lasting message of resilience and making it against all odds.

In many ways, my life has been a living "Sí, se puede" story.

I think my mother tried to convey the same message to my sister and me, but using a different expression: "Pa' lante y pa' encima. Pa' atrás, ni para coger impulso," meaning "Going forward, being on, and not looking behind, not even to gain momentum." She repeated this expression time and time again, even while coping with PD. Today, I remind my daughters of *Abuelita*'s adage to always move forward. And although they understand and acknowledge its meaning, my daughters also remind me how much grandma loved Daddy Yankee's "Gasolina" reggaeton song, which could be interpreted as another way to continue moving forward. My mother knew that gasoline, just as it can power a car, can symbolize the energy behind someone's life choices like a driving force, a call of "Sí, se puede."

I planned on always moving forward but I didn't plan on becoming a leader. Creating or developing a leadership approach that would take me to the highest levels of government was never my goal as a child or young woman growing up in Puerto Rico in the 1970s and '80s. I studied sociology with the intention to become culturally aware, to understand and engage with a tapestry of cultures. I never thought that it would lead me to leadership positions.

Yet, somehow, my life trajectory led me there. Sociology whispers from college professors Jaime Gutierrez and Manuel Valdes Pizzini showed me the way to acknowledging and respecting differences, and helped me develop the necessary skills to effectively interact with people from diverse backgrounds.

Leaders like Ambassador Lino Gutierrez, Postmaster Joe Rivera, and career SES Felicita Sola-Carter saw a spark in my eyes and, believing in my potential, took me under their wing, helping me learn the basics of leadership.

Government jobs representing the United States taught me about duty, honor, and the responsibility to uphold democratic values and principles. Secretaries Colin Powell, Hillary Clinton, and Deb Haaland showed me the significance of empathy, emotional intelligence, collaboration, and self-awareness, alongside authenticity.

And then there is my family: my parents, Anibal and Zoraida; my sister Vicky; my husband Carlos and our daughters Ashley, Amanda and Adriana. They believed in me all along, showed me their love and support, and helped me build my confidence and resilience.

In the process of learning to become a leader, there were no straight lines, just a "Sí, se puede" attitude. I gained knowledge and skills by reading, taking courses, and observing other leaders, both good and bad ones. I knew that excellent leadership meant treating individuals with dignity and respect, being genuine and authentic, and leading by example. Above all, it required persevering through challenges, and believe me, there were plenty!

From working through a pandemic while losing my mother and other close family members, to supporting my daughter with her mental health struggles and being treated differently because of my accent, gender, or status as a civil service employee, these challenges only motivated me to work harder and chase my passions. While I grew up with limited resources, I came to see this adversity not as obstruction, but instruction. The setbacks I encountered were opportunities to learn valuable life lessons, helping me identify my strengths and weaknesses, acquire problem-solving skills, and maintain a flexible way of thinking. Along the way, I was building resilience.

Finding the bright side when times were tough was not easy, especially when I was far away from family while serving in the FSM during the pandemic. But as I learned, bouncing back is crucial to making sound decisions, guiding teams through unpredictable times, and inspiring confidence in others. If you can stay calm and focused, motivate your team, and foster a culture of growth by viewing adversity as an opportunity to learn and improve, you will create an organization capable of thriving in difficult situations. Having to manage complicated situations also taught me that I had the responsibility to guide, inspire, and motivate others by creating supportive environments where everyone feels empowered to contribute.

In 2022, this and many other bits of advice were compiled by a friend and *hermana* from the National Hispana Leadership Institute, Delia Garcia, in her book *Latina Leadership Lessons*. She asked fifty women leaders from all over the United States to share their nuggets of wisdom. I was honored to be featured.

"Sí, se puede" was the guiding principle behind all my endeavors, especially during my time in public service. It's an honor and privilege to serve the public, and when you do, you are able to effect change in policies and contribute to communities, making a difference in the process. Merit-based, non-partisan government work protects our democracy and can offer a sense of purpose and fulfillment, knowing that your efforts directly impact the lives of others. That mindset underpinned everything I did.

I was appointed to two high-level positions in the US government by two Presidents from opposing political parties. I became the eleventh US ambassador and one of a small number of assistant secretaries originating from Puerto Rico. I feel privileged to have served in three presidential appointments, an honor that I never imagined growing up in Mayagüez. I also feel very fortunate that I got to work with so many leaders who showed me the way, from Secretary of State Colin Powell, who underscored the importance of strong moral character, to Secretary of the Interior Deb Haaland, who highlighted the importance of never repeating history's worst mistakes

But spending a few hours with Dolores Huerta in my office in September 2012 became an unexpected gift, an informal mentoring session where I absorbed her wisdom like a sponge. That day, Dolores talked about the significance of not giving up and bringing someone with you along the way. She stressed the importance of taking action and speaking up, and shared some of her regrets, including how she felt after Senator Robert F. Kennedy (RFK) was gunned down in California in 1968, wondering if she could have done more to prevent this tragic event from happening. [100]

When one speaks up and their voice is heard, change becomes possible. You can inspire others who may have been hesitant to share their insights, and open doors for those who might have been waiting for someone else to show the way. Learning all this from Dolores, who at ninety-five continues to be a source of inspiration, was a blessing. Most importantly, Dolores reminded me that what we do is part of a long journey, not a quick moment.

"Sí, se puede" is a shining reflection of resilience. Whatever it is that you want to do in life, I encourage you to follow your guiding light. Your path, like mine, can be a "Sí, se puede" story. And as Mami would say, "Pa' lante y pa' encima, pa' atras ni para coger impulso!"

---

[100] In 1968, Dolores Huerta was escorting RFK to a press conference in a ballroom when they were instructed to go to the kitchen instead, something not previously planned. This is where the Senator was shot.

Epilogue: Island Duchess

Pencil drawing by Adriana Cantor of
Carmen G. Cantor
2020

I had spent two hours sitting on the floor, watching a traditional Pohnpeian ceremony with all sorts of offerings pigs, fruits, and sakau when the paramount chief of the island of Pohnpei, the king of kings, the *Nahnmwarki* (king) of Madolenihmw, made an announcement that sent a collective gasp through the *nahs*, the ceremonial meeting house in the village. At first, I did not understand what was happening. The king, wearing his traditional Micronesian attire, something I was told did not happen often, made his declaration as the sky opened up and a torrential downpour began.

I had arrived in Pohnpei, one of the wettest places on Earth, FSM, six months earlier. I had made it one of my priorities to strengthen the relationship between the US and the FSM, and spent a significant amount of time meeting with host government officials on a variety of matters such as (economic assistance, defense, telecommunications, health, education, sustainability, and human rights, among other topics) while also assisting US citizens with individual concerns. As a new ambassador, I wanted to fortify the bond between the two nations by promoting open communication. That meant getting to know the country better by meeting its citizens and traditional leaders in their villages, building people-to-people connections that fostered mutual understanding, respect, and trust.

The Micronesians were delighted that a woman from Puerto Rico had been appointed as the US President's representative to their young island nation. They knew that someone coming from another island would understand the challenges they were facing better than others. However, my understanding of the FSM before being nominated as US ambassador in mid-July of 2019 was somewhat shallow. My knowledge of countries in the Western Hemisphere was first-hand, current, and comprehensive. I was less informed about countries in Asia and the Pacific.

As time progressed, I learned about the FSM's politics, traditions, and history including the fact that the Nahnmwarki, who made the proclamation in the nahs, was a direct descendant of the Saudeleurs, the dynasty that ruled over the peoples of Pohnpei until around 1628.

When I first arrived in Pohnpei in January 2020, the staff at the embassy was very welcoming. They were curious about Puerto Rico and asked an abundance of questions about my home island. I didn't realize until a few weeks later that the interest was based on their fascination with another *Boricua* singer and actress, Jennifer Lopez, who was scheduled to co-headline the Super Bowl half-time show in early February, along with Colombian singer Shakira.

The people of the FSM love American football. Most national and state government offices in Pohnpei do not open when a big game is on. The Super Bowl is played on a Sunday evening in the US but due to the sixteen-hour time difference, it airs on a Monday morning in the FSM. In 2020, the San Francisco 49ers played the Kansas City Chiefs, and the Chiefs ended up winning 31-20. Pohnpeians were thrilled about Kansas City's victory, because there is a significant Micronesian population in the Kansas City area, especially from the island of Pohnpei. With time, I gained a better understanding of the Micronesian diaspora in the US and their passion for football, baseball, and tennis.

The embassy staff was ecstatic to meet someone from JLo's island. They asked me about Puerto Rico's music, climate, and traditional cuisine. My office management specialist, Emmerlynn Shed, in particular, was a huge fan of the singer. Months later, I discerned that, for many, including Emmerlynn, I was not only the first islander from outside the Pacific region they were meeting, but also the first Puerto Rican or Latina they ever met.

By the way, everyone at the embassy was thrilled with JLo's Super Bowl half-time show performance.

Fast-forward six months, and I'm sitting in the nahs of the Nahnmwarki, a few miles from the Saudeleurs' center of power, Nan Madol the only ancient city in the world built on top of a coral reef in a lagoon. There I was, 8,800 miles from my native Mayagüez, Puerto Rico, attending a traditional Pohnpeian ceremony under a deluge of rain, something seen as a blessing in Pohnpeian culture a symbol of prosperity and renewal.

That morning, before departing the US Embassy in Kolonia, my driver Soster was pumped about our trip to the municipality of Madolenihmw. Abby Kim, my public diplomacy assistant, a locally employed staff member, tried to explain to me the protocols of how Pohnpeian traditional ceremonies worked. She said: "If offered sakau, close your eyes while you drink from the coconut cup. Keep your eyes shut until you remove it from your lips."

I asked about sakau. Abby explained that it was a communal drink, made from the root of the pepper shrub, pounded on a basalt stone, and then squeezed through the inner bark of a hibiscus tree. She said it symbolized the island's traditional culture and was used to socialize and relax. What she didn't tell me is that immediately after you drink it, it makes your mouth completely numb. (My face after my first sip later that day must have betrayed the shock, as someone quickly offered me coconut water. The numbness disappears a few minutes later if you only drink a few sips, which became the norm every time I was offered it).

Abby then proceeded to describe the order of the ceremony I was about to be part of: The first sakau cup goes to the Nahnmwarki, then it follows the line of succession, going to the *Nahnke* and then to the *Nahnalik*, before returning to the Nahnmwarki. During the process, the *Menindei* (a host or master of ceremonies) imparts the Nahnmwarki's orders to the people and announces the purpose of the gathering.

The atmosphere in the nahs was festive. Before the traditional ceremony started, the brother of the Nahnmwarki, a US Navy veteran who spent many years of his life in the Pohnpeian diaspora in Kansas City, asked me to dance. Herbert Hebel held the title of *Wasahi*. An avid American football and baseball fan, he moved back to Pohnpei with his wife in 2019 to fulfill his duty as a member of the royal dynasty in Madolenihmw. The Wasahi was happy to be back in Pohnpei and told me he was proud of his military service as a member of the US Navy. He loved the United States and appreciated how the values of the two countries aligned.

After the dance, the moment came for the Nahnmwarki to give remarks to the two-hundred-plus people present. His address was in Pohnpeian, one of the native tongues spoken in the country. Knowing that I did not understand the language, Lynn Pangelinan, one of the political assistants at the embassy, sat on the floor next to me and simultaneously interpreted as the speech was given. The Nahnmwarki discussed people-to-people connections and the importance of the US-FSM relationship, before concluding his remarks. The late Majesty Wasa Lapalap Isopahu Kerpet Hebel then bestowed a traditional title on me: *Nahnei Isopahu*.

That's when everyone in the room inhaled in unison, their mouths open in astonishment! Lynn turned to me and said: "Ambassador, you have just been given a very high title by the Nahnmwarki. You are now a member of his own family, Isopahu. It's like being named a duchess, like in the English Royal Family!"

At first, I was flabbergasted. Traditional titles in Pohnpei are given to men and women based on birth right, marriage, and, in instances like mine, achievements. Never in my life had I dreamed of being recognized with such an honor by the citizens of another country. But this was not an isolated incident. Not long after the ceremony in Madolenihmw, two other traditional chiefs bestowed titles upon me:. The king of the municipality of Kitti in Pohnpei, the late Majesty Wasa Lapalap Soukisehleng Nahnmwarki, Gregorio Peter, conferred on me the title *Nahnei Dierensapw*.[101] The king and queen of the municipality of Nett, His Royal Highness Isonahnken Salvador Iriarte and Her Royal Highness Nahnkeniei Ruth Iriarte, awarded me the title *Soumadau En Doulik Lapalap Nett*.[102]

---

[101] *Nahnei Dierensapw* means woman from a tiny island that often forms into something bigger.

[102] *Soumadau En Doulik Lapalap* could translate to Great Warrior Chief of Doulik of the municipality of Nett.

Who would have thought that someone like me would be bestowed with noble titles by Pohnpeian traditional leaders as a way to officially recognize my work?

The local staff at the embassy were very proud of the titles and spoke of them often. What I didn't know until near the end of my tenure in the FSM, is that the staff had struggled with finding a fitting call sign or name for me the entire time I worked in Pohnpei. The embassy team was very respectful and always followed protocols, especially when it came to using the title of ambassador or chief of mission. Eventually, I learned that some in the local security forces and members of the Defense Attaché Office referred to me as "Duchess of Nan Madol" or "Nahnei" when speaking amongst themselves. I also learned that some local staff wanted to use "JLo" because of my Puerto Rican heritage or "Carminator" this last one because of my relentless pursuit of finishing what I start. Ultimately, Duchess was the call name that stuck. And so, I became Nahnei or Island Duchess, US Ambassador to the FSM.

It meant everything to be seen, embraced, and crowned as family. The journey began in Mayagüez fifty-seven years ago, and somehow it led here. Bestowed titles not by power, but by trust. Not for where I came from, but for how I showed up.

In the end, that's the legacy I cherish most.

ABOUT THE AUTHOR

 Ambassador Carmen G. Cantor most recently served as the Assistant Secretary for Insular and International Affairs at the U.S. Department of the Interior, where she oversaw the Department's responsibilities regarding the U.S. territories, freely associated states, international technical engagement, and the oceans, Great Lakes, and coasts. Previously, she served as U.S. Ambassador Extraordinary and Plenipotentiary to the Federated States of Micronesia and in various roles within the Department of State, including as the Executive Director of the Bureau of Educational and Cultural Affairs and Bureau of International Information Programs, Executive Director of the Bureau of Counterterrorism, Director of the Office of Civil Service Human Resource Management and as Deputy Director for Recruitment, Examination, and Employment. In her over three decades of public service, Ambassador Cantor also served as Director of the Office of Civil Rights for the Foreign Agricultural Service, and as Director of the

Office of Equal Employment Opportunity at the Federal Maritime Commission. Ambassador Cantor was born in Puerto Rico and raised in the city of Mayagüez, where she earned a B.A. from the University of Puerto Rico and then an M.A. from the Inter-American University of Puerto Rico. She has a certificate in International Migration Studies from Georgetown University School of Continuing Studies. Ambassador Cantor is married and has three grown children.